FREE TO BE ME

The Raw Musings of a Woman Unbound

"This book is a memoir, based on true events..."

"This memoir is based on my personal experiences. While the events depicted are true, some names, locations, and character traits have been changed for privacy reasons. Dialogue and some details have been recreated from memory."

Written by:

Patricia Morrison-Collins

Disclaimers:
Errors or inconsistencies you may come across were intentionally retained from the original manuscript to preserve the author's authentic voice and style.

Prepared for Publication by:
Vonda Almond

Book Cover Art by
Jordan Rylee Collins Almond

Copyright © 2025
By Patricia Morrison-Collins
(Egatireh)

ISBN: 9798285411024
Imprint: Independently Published

Forward

This book is more than just a story—it's a raw and honest glimpse into a real life lived with intensity, struggle, and resilience. From the very first page, I was pulled into the author's world. Her experiences—both heartbreaking and uplifting—felt so vividly real that it was impossible not to be deeply moved.

The twists throughout the book were unexpected and kept me completely engaged. Just when I thought I understood where her journey was going, another layer was revealed, often challenging my assumptions and deepening my empathy.

What makes this book stand out is its emotional depth. You don't just read about her pain—you feel it. The loneliness, the fear, the injustice, but also the fierce hope and small victories. And when happiness does come, it feels earned and real, like you're sharing a quiet triumph with someone you've come to know personally.

This isn't just a memoir; it's a testimony to human strength and vulnerability. I walked away from it not just entertained, but changed. Highly recommended for anyone who loves true stories that are rich, layered, and unforgettable.

Mrs. Jessica Kelley, M.Ed. 5th Grade Teacher

Preface

I never realized how hard it is just to get a publisher to read a person's writing until now; of course, I never tried until the last few years. I had written just for myself as a way to express all the questions I had, especially about my father. In October 1992, I found him, my father.

He was 77, and I was 50. I lost him to this world in November 1994. We had two years together, and I learned what it was to feel "free to be me," the title of my story.

So when I bought my first computer and then the web, I saw a way to get my story told. It might take me the rest of my life to put a few pages at a time on my homepage, but at least there might be someone out there to learn something from it about
love, family, and the importance
of faith in Jesus Christ.

Reviews in their entirety

Raw, emotional, and deeply introspective, this book offers a heartfelt glimpse into Patricia's life and faith. She shares how Jesus—her Lord and Savior—was protecting and guiding her long before she fully gave her life to Him. Through her story, we witness a woman wrestling with the pain of abandonment and ultimately finding peace with those who hurt her deeply. It's an inspiring testimony of healing, resilience, and the transformative power of faith, as Patricia openly invites us into the moments that shaped her life and the decisions that defined her journey.

Pamela Mckinney - Paraeducator/LAP Reading Intervention

This collection is a heartfelt journey through the life of a woman whose story is stitched together with love, surprises, honesty, and deeply genuine moments. Each page offers a glimpse into the emotional tapestry of a life fully lived, celebrating its joys and confronting its challenges with grace and raw truth. The author's voice is warm and reflective, making this memoir not just a personal recollection but a relatable testament to the beauty of everyday experience. It's a touching tribute to resilience, love, and the quiet strength that defines a woman's heart.

Jessica Clark - 5th grade Teacher

Acknowledgements

This book, a tribute to my mother's life and legacy, would not have been possible without the invaluable contributions of several individuals who supported me in unique ways.

Jessica Clark: For the suggestion of the subtitle, "The Raw Musings of a Woman Unbound." It perfectly captures the essence of my mom's story.
As well as navigating the intricacies of self-publishing.

Jessica Kelley: For guidance on copyright legalities. Your input on self-publishing, especially concerning intellectual property, was made significantly smoother thanks to your expertise.

Pam McKinney: For encouragement and providing the vital information that ultimately brought this book to fruition. Belief in this project and practical advice were instrumental in overcoming obstacles and maintaining motivation.

Finally, thanks to everyone who encouraged me to embark on the journey of self-publishing my mother's memoir. Enthusiasm and support made a world of difference during challenging moments and fueled the determination to share this story.

Free, To be Me

October 20, 1992, I was at my night supervisory position. It was seven p.m. It had been a quiet night, so far. I heard my name paged over the intercom that I had a call. I figured it was probably a family member of one of our residents. I picked up the receiver and said, "East View, Mrs. Colan speaking can I help you." My husband's voice said, "It's just me." I immediately jumped to the conclusion that something must be wrong. He quickly assured me saying, "Nothing is wrong, I think this is good I just spoke to your father." It had been 41 years since I had seen or spoke to my father.

This is the story of not only finding my father, but also finding myself. It all began in the spring of 1938 at the Gateway in Minneapolis, Minnesota.

A tall, browned eyed twenty-four-year-old man had just hopped off a freight train, as it pulled into the Minneapolis depot. He had been riding the rails for some time. He was tired, hungry and broke.

Minneapolis was not a stranger to this young man. He headed to an- area that, from previous experience, he knew he could get a real meal and a warm cot for the night.

The Gateway was an area where Hennepin and Nicolette Avenues came together forming a triangle. The Gateway area in the late 19th century was the hub of the city's labor supply for the major railroad lines in the upper Midwest. Therefore, it had become a stopping off place for the freight-hoppers.

The Gateway building was on Washington Avenue. Washington avenue ran North and South across the far end of the triangle formed by Hennepin and Nicolette. The main entrance on Washington, consisted of a travelers' aid information bureau for the city of Minneapolis. In the basement were public restrooms. There was a park that joined the Gateway building where the townspeople, travelers, and drifters gathered in the spring and summer. About a block or so from the Gateway building and the park was the Mississippi river that separated St. Paul from Minneapolis. Along Hennepin and Nicolette Avenues were bars, hotels, bakeries, barber shops and a place that sold fresh squeezed juices and a couple cafes.

In one such cafe this young man entered to order a cup of coffee. He was tired and hungry. The waitress who waited on him had just recently entered through the Gateway herself. She was a beautiful blue eyed country girl from a small town approximately one hundred miles from Minneapolis. She was eighteen years old and just out of high school. The young man's name was Mike and the waitress' name was Lettie.

Mike ordered his cup of coffee. He came back a number of times, each time without enough money to buy anything to eat, usually just a cup of coffee. But there was always a little something extra with his coffee. One time the waitress told Mike to sit in a booth and brought him a whole meal: two eggs, hash browns, toast and coffee. Mike said, "I did not order this." The waitress said, "Shut up and eat it. " In the late thirties a meal like this would cost approximately fifteen cents.

There was no way these two young people could

have ever guessed about the future, and the profound effect they had on my life.

It didn't take long before Mike realized that something was being stirred inside him, that he was not ready for, a commitment to another human being. Lettie also was becoming serious about this young man. Mike felt that it might be best if he disappeared, so he told Lettie that he was leaving town. But he didn't go very far, and a few weeks later he was with a couple other guys on a street corner. The next thing he knew Lettie was standing in front of him. Lettie said, "Mike when did you get back in town?" The surprising thing to Mike was how he felt when he saw her. He finally had to admit that this woman was not just another one night stand. He was in love with her. Shortly after this realization, Mike was over in the St. Paul area and was picked up for vagrancy. A person picked up for vagrancy is held for twenty-four hours and then told to leave town. There was only one person that Mike knew, so he called Lettie. When she showed up, Mike tried not to laugh, for her hair was no longer blond, but very red.

She told him that she wanted a change. Mike moved in with Lettie

Both of these people had more in common than the love between a man and woman. Their zest for life, their tenderness and sensitivity, plus their search for something to put meaning and purpose in their lives brought them even closer. These two special people became my Mom and Dad.

Mom was adopted when she was two years old. When she was ten, the only mother she ever had died. Her father remarried just a few years later. Mom's new stepmother was just three years older than herself, and with a baby. Mom had to help with the care of the baby. It didn't take long before she became resentful of her new duties. As soon as she graduated from High School, as Valedictorian of her graduation class, she left Avon.

Dad never knew his father, he died before he was born. His grandfather, on his mother's side, was the only one to whom he felt close. His grandfather died before Dad met Mom. He had a stepfather that he didn't get along with. By the time Dad was sixteen he was hopping freight trains.

When he was about nineteen, late one night, he and a friend broke into the town pool hall. They took some candy, cigarettes, and anything that was just laying around, there was no money to take. A few days later they were both caught. Dad got two years in the state penitentiary. After eleven months, he escaped. A year later, when he went to see his Mother, he was rearrested and put back where he had been before. Two months later he escaped again. He stayed on the run, until he met Mom.

Mom and Dad married July 21, 1940, in Minneapolis. Because of Mom, Dad began to want to change his life. Dad went to work as a chauffeur for Roger Wills. Dad drove for Mr. Wills for a few weeks and then asked if he could borrow the car to take Mom to see her family. Mr. Wills said okay, so Dad and Mom went for a visit and was introduced to his new in-laws. Well, Mr. Wills and Dad became friends, but Dad still didn't know anything about his business. Dad was getting a paycheck and that was all that mattered until a trip to Omaha, Nebraska.

One night in Omaha Dad was in his hotel room when a knock on the door woke him up. Two policemen arrested him and took him to jail, where he found out that Mr. Wills was a con man. After a few days the police were convinced that Dad had not known what was going on. A bigger problem faced him now, He was broke, and in Omaha and Mom was in Minneapolis. Dad said a minister came to the jail and gave Dad a bus ticket to Kansas City, Missouri, and told him that his wife would be waiting for him there. Mom in the meantime went to work at the Schuyler Hotel as a switchboard operator, and had rented a room from a Emma Mason. Dad caught that bus and Mom met him just as the minister told him she would.

By the time I was born dad had gone to work at the Schuyler Hotel, and his salary included an apartment. So they left Emma's and moved into the Schuyler. Emma remained a lifetime friend of moms.

December 18, 1941, I entered this world at 7:24 a.m. I was named Patricia, but I have always been called Patty by my mother and father. I was baptized on January 11, 1942, at Saint Patrick's Church in Kansas City, Missouri.

For some reason mom had a difficult time, finally a cesarean section had to be done. I can imagine what my father looked like. The same tall brown eyed man that just a few years earlier had been jumping off freight trains, with no roots and no responsibilities, was pacing the floor at St. Mary's Hospital in Kansas City, waiting and wondering how things were going. Unlike fathers today that have a front row seat at the birth of their children, fathers back then had to wait and worry. Dad has never mentioned in our talks if he had a preference for a son or a daughter. But no matter what he wanted once he saw me it must have been love at first sight. I believe that what transpired between this tiny daughter and her father was something that time couldn't destroy.

Mom nursed me until I was nine months old, holding me, singing to me, looking into the same brown eyes of my father, each time she looked at me. For Mom, I think that was part of the beauty and later it became a painful reminder. Each time she looked into my eyes, she saw the eyes of the first and only true love she was to ever have. And as I grew older, it was plain to see that I was so much like my father.

Dad's brown eyes would twinkle, as he would pick me up and look into brown eyes so much like his. This tall handsome man I believe conveyed such a sensitivity to his daughter, that even now when I look at those big hands that at one time held me, I have a sense of that small baby as she was held by him. Even then there was a bond between this father and daughter. He would take me with him, around the hotel where he worked and we lived. And to the neighborhood stores with a pride that only a father can know. It must have been the happiest days of their lives. At last, they had found what they were searching for, or at least they thought it was at the time. Their love for each other and a daughter born of that love.

The first sixteen months of my life was probably the most important and for sure the most stable part of my life for many, many years. When I say the most important part of my life, it's because through research, society found that the first three years of a child's life including the period before birth will have a profound effect on that life.

Dad has told me what he remembers of those first sixteen months of our lives together. Dad remembers a trip that the three of us took to Minnesota, to the farm. We went by bus, Dad said the one thing that stands out in his memory was how good I was, never crying. Mom told me a story about a trip we took to the farm. I don't know if it was the time that Dad remembers or not. Anyway, as Mom told me she had been raised in the Catholic church by her parents. It was a Sunday morning, and she had let her parents think that Dad was a Catholic. Therefore, he was expected to go to church just as the rest of the family and being a dutiful son-in-law and Catholic, he went. It was my grandfather's custom to sit on the front seat of the church, and of course Mom and Dad sat there as well. For those that don't know, during a Catholic service there are times when the congregation stands, sits and kneels. For a

Catholic this was no problem, but for my six foot, four inch father it was. It didn't take long for grandpa to figure out that his son-in-law was not a Catholic. Later after this incident he was baptized and married Mom in the Catholic church.

When I was about sixteen months old, Dad joined the Army. Our government, during the war, was offering pardons in return for enlisting in the military and Dad had been using an alias, James Michael Ryan, until he met Mom. The Army gave Dad a chance to put the past behind him. This way our family wouldn't have to worry about his past. The choice at the time was right, there was no way to see the future. No way to see what would happen to their love. No way to see the effects this separation would cause.

Dad was gone thirty-three months. There were letters and pictures sent to him and also letters from him. I remember a record that was sent by Dad from overseas where he called Mom pumpkin and talked about his little Patty and his love for us and how much he missed us.

Back here at night, with Dad gone, those big gentle hands no longer held me. I no longer was able to see the twinkle in his eyes and see my own eyes reflected back at me. Something had changed, as a child I didn't understand, I just knew that my life was no longer the same.

Mom, I think because of her constant need to have somebody make her feel special, and her own insecurities from her childhood just couldn't handle the separation. Mike was not there to remind her how much she was loved and needed. As much as she loved me, I couldn't take the place of Dad. The nights when she was alone and longed for the arms of her love around her was just too much.

I don't know when, but sometime within those thirty-three months that Dad was gone she started looking for security and love with someone else. I'm sure that each time she would hold me, she would be reminded of Dad. The one thing that she, at one time was so pleased with, the resemblance between me and Dad, now was only a painful reminder that he wasn't there.

I don't remember, at least consciously, those days, the long days and months that Dad was gone. The only thing I have to go by now, forty-seven years later, from the time Dad was discharged from the army is what he has told me, and bits and pieces that Mom said when I was a child. How much of what Mom said is factual I don't know. Because of the emotional problems that led to her drinking problem, her ability to see things as they really were, was probably cloudy.

Sometime during those months that Dad was gone, Mom moved us from the Schuyler Hotel to an apartment in the building that belonged to Emma Mason.

December 1945, Dad was discharged after being in the South Pacific. He was sent to Seattle, Washington and from there to Fort Leavenworth, Kansas. Before going to Leavenworth, he came to Kansas City and spent a day or two with Mom and me. During his couple days with us Mom introduced him to a friend that she had made. His name was Cecil Pence. Then Dad went on to Leavenworth for seven to ten days till final discharge. At that time there was no hint of anything wrong, as far as Dad knew. About ten days later Dad came home for good. I had turned four years old the eighteenth day of December.

When Dad came back from Fort Leavenworth, he was told that Mom didn't want to see him anymore. Dad says he doesn't remember who it was that gave him the message, but he thinks it was a woman. That two days he spent with us was the last time he saw Mom. After receiving Mom's message, Dad went back to the Schuyler Hotel and got his old job back.

What seems so strange to me is where was I, didn't anybody consider how I felt? Did I see Dad that day? Did I cry or did I at that time begin to retreat to a place within myself where no one could hurt me? They had taught me and showed me love and then seemed to forget me. Mom couldn't forget me, she just forgot what was important. Did I know that the "friend" of Mom's would be my substitute father? I remember calling Cecil daddy, but it wasn't the same. From that time, this little girl hid a hurt that would take forty-six years to heal. Mom gave me anything that money could buy, but what I needed didn't cost a thing.

Mom told me sometime before I turned ten that Dad had left her for another woman, and that she had talked to her and told her to leave Dad. She also told me that this woman was wealthy. And in the conversation with this other woman she was told, "you can't squeeze blood out of a turnip" and Mom said, "that blood is thicker than water," till this day I still don't understand the conversation that was supposed to have taken place. According to Mom, her and Dad divorced when I was two, shortly after he returned from the army. I now realize that things were not always as Mom said.

Dad met Loran at the Schuyler and remarried the following April. Mom married Cecil around this time as well. Again, there was one person's feelings in all this that was not considered, that four-and-a-half-year-old. But she never forgot that she, at one time had a mother and father, who at one time had loved each other and their daughter.

I spent a couple Sundays with Dad and Loran after they married. Dad has told me what he remembers about those days. Mom was never there when he picked me up, and when he took me home, I would cry and say,

"Don't want to go to mommy home." Dad says I was very quiet and withdrawn, for the most part. I have no memories of those days. Because of the hurt of not having my parents together, and other emotional factors, I believe that those memories have been buried deeply in my subconscious.

At fifty-one, I think of that little girl, and it's almost as if she is someone, that I have to protect against being hurt again. Her Mom had a new husband, and a new exciting life. Her Dad had a new wife and a new son. The little girl was left without anybody to help her understand what had happened to her family.

From the time I was five until I was ten is so vague, that I have only dim memories that seem more like a very distant dream. I remember times that my resemblance to Dad would make Mom angry. If I would do something that would displease her, she would say, "You're just like your Dad."

There were good times and bad times. In the summer we would go to Avon, Minnesota to the farm where Mom grew up. Avon and the farm have always held fond memories for me. The large white framed two-story farmhouse. A large back and front porch where quilting and churning of the cream into butter took place along with a number of other things. The barn down behind the house, the hay loft and the lake that stretched out from behind the barn. The lake shore around the two hundred forty acres of farmland, where I would spend time walking, where Mom walked as a child, and enjoying the solitude and beauty. I would talk to the big friendly brown eyed cows about all those feelings of a very lonely child with no one to talk to or give any answers to. I would spend time fishing, or I would take the rowboat out into the middle of the lake drop anchor and fish or sometimes just sit and daydream.

In kindergarten I would cry so easy that the other kids would tease me, calling me names like "fatty patty." I was so timid and so alone, so afraid of getting hurt.

I remember skating on the sidewalk in front of the building in which we lived. I remember once when I was about six or seven letting some bigger boy talk me in to playing chicken with him. I was to stand with my legs apart and he would see how close to my feet he could throw his knife. He got closer than he intended to, Mom or Cecil had to pull the knife out through my shoe, foot, and the ground.

One Christmas morning I woke up and under the tree was a whole toy kitchen set up; a toy stove, a refrigerator, table and chairs, a new highchair with a beautiful new doll in it. Also, there were new clothes and stockings full of goodies. But all the things in the world didn't make me happy, I was still a very sad and lonely child.

Emma Mason owned a farm close to Dora, Missouri. In the summers I would spend three or four weeks there. Riding the horses was my favorite thing to do. I enjoyed it there like I did the farm in Minnesota.

I remember a time when Cecil's father came for a visit. I remember telling Mom and Cecil that he had touched me where he shouldn't, and it scared me. Cecil told his father to leave and never to come back. I never saw him again.

One special time I remember was a night I walked into Mom and Cecil's bedroom. They were in bed and making love. At the age of nine I didn't understand what was going on. I ran out of the bedroom scared. Mom, about fifteen minutes later came into my bedroom. She told me that someday I would fall in love and get married, and the love between my husband and myself would be expressed in a special closeness, a physical closeness. She told me that kind of love should not take place until I was married. This was the Mother I loved.

I also remember when I was nine. I reached into our clothes closet and bumped something; it was glass. I pulled it out and found it to be a half empty whiskey bottle.

The year I turned ten, 1951, was the year I remember the most. The incident that made this year a time I always remembered lasted only, at the most ten minutes. It was summer during school vacation. Mom and Cecil were at work, and I was at home alone. Mom had always told me never to open the door unless I was sure of who it was.

There was a knock on the door, without thinking I opened the door. Standing in the door was this very tall, handsome, browned eyed man. I remember thinking how big he was. I just stood there looking up at him. He said looking at me, "Patty?" I don't remember making a comment, nodding my head or anything, but I do remember the pounding of my heart. I knew I should know this man. " Is your mother home?" he asked. I think I said, " No, she's at work. " The next thing He said was, " Patty, I'm your father. " This was not a stranger, this was my daddy. Oh, how I wanted him to reach out and put his arms around his little girl. I wanted to be held by my father I wasn't a baby anymore, but I had never stopped missing my father's love.

He never came into the apartment. He stood there in the doorway and told me about his stepson, and that they lived on a lake and how he would like for me to come and visit with him and meet his stepson, William. I don't remember saying anything else to him. He said something about a check for Mom and then turned and left, taking part of my heart with him. He never knew how I felt about him, not until forty years later.

That night Mom came home from work, as she came through the door, I said, " My Daddy was here and he asked me to come and see him, he was so nice. " Mom became very angry, spanked me and told me that I was never to mention his name again. I never mentioned his name again to her, but I never forgot either.

I remember an incident I had almost forgot. I don't know what preceded this incident, I only know that I was a very unhappy and lonely girl. I ran away from home one night, Mom and Cecil found me on twelfth street, about three blocks from home. I was taken home and was given a whipping, with no questions asked or answers given. Mom's drinking was getting worse and sometime within the following year; Mom came home and found Cecil in their bed with a "friend" of hers. I was at the babysitters upstairs.

Mom and I moved to Minnesota. We were there only a year. Mom worked in Minneapolis. I wonder now if Mom ever visited the Gateway area, where she meant Dad, while she lived there.

I lived with my grandfather and Florence, Mom's stepmother on the farm. I spent most of my sixth grade in Avon, at a school that had one teacher for every four grades of school. It was quite a change from the city schools. Every moment that was not spent with chores, was spent on the lake in the boat, walking in the pastures, or just sitting or lying on the grass thinking about the future. Sometimes I'd hide in the hay loft, so I could be by myself. What would become of me? Where would I go? I wanted to do something that would be worth something to somebody someday. I would daydream of a family, a Mom, a Dad, and a brother or a sister.

I guess I was a real dreamer. Many of my dreams have come true and some have not. As the years have gone by, my dreams seem to be taking on a new dimension that goes beyond this life and into eternity.

Florence became very angry with me because of my moods and the solitude that would lock out everything and everybody. Always retreating into my own little world. She would write Mom or complain to Mom about my attitude. Mom would tell me to straighten up and get along with Florence. These moods of mine have always been difficult for others to deal with.

Sometime during my twelfth year, we moved back to Kansas City. We moved into a brick apartment building, across from where we had lived during Mom's marriage to Cecil, called the "Chimes." Mom was drinking pretty heavy but still working. About this time something happened to me. I quit being the sweet little quiet girl. I no longer dreamed of the future.

I began to see that my dreams were just a figment of my imagination. I would never have the family I wanted so badly. Never have anybody that would look at me and see someone special. I found that if I talked big enough and loud enough and showed how tough I was, no one would hurt me anymore. The dreams and tears were gone. I would show the world I didn't need anybody.

I had made friends, a few just as tough as I thought I was, and one that was totally different. I don't remember her name now, but she introduced me to a life I had never seen, and at the time didn't want. She asked me to go to church with her and out of curiosity I went. It was a small church, with a small congregation. The people sang, clapped their hands and had what they called "the spirit." I remember a man at the altar praying. I always thought prayer was something you recited from memory. This man was praying out loud and like he was talking to somebody. I told my friend that they were crazy fanatics and left. I never had much to do with her after that, but years later I would remember her.

Nellie Gillis and her brother were part of the new group of friends I made. Their parents were divorced also. Gene, her brother, became my first boyfriend. We began to make out. I enjoyed holding each other and kissing, but that was as far as I would go.

Nellie and I would play hooky and hang out in downtown Kansas City. There was a problem with our friendship, Nellie was a real beauty, so I always got the boys she didn't want, which didn't help myself esteem any. I never felt attractive. Never could believe that anybody could see anything in me, but I couldn't blame them much since I couldn't see anything either.

I started running around with some tougher girls who were less attractive than me. This improved my chances with the boys and also made the girls look up to me more. We would steal gas caps, cut tires, anything for a kick. When we could get it, we would see how much we could drink. I started smoking and bleached my hair. Nobody ever guessed that under this thirteen-year-old, hard acting, bleached blond was a love starved kid, that was sure there was nothing lovable about her.

One night, a friend of mine and I were out walking the streets, bored and looking for excitement. Two guys in a fancy, souped up car pulled up beside us and said, " How about a ride." We looked at each other and into the car we jumped. It wasn't long before we realized that we had jumped into the wrong car. They took us down to the west bottoms by the Missouri River. The guy I was with started trying to push me back and his hands were trying to go places I didn't want them to go. I kept saying, "No, stop." He just got rougher and said, " What did you expect?" I found the door handle and managed to open it and fell out of the car. My friend in the front seat was having trouble but also managed to get out of the car. The guys hollered at us, as they drove away, "Okay... Walk." We were stranded a couple miles from home late at night, and neither one of us was about to call our parents. So, we took off walking. It took us close to a hour to get home, but we made it okay. I would like to say that I had learned my lesson, but I didn't. I just sized people up more, became tougher, and learned how to be street smart.

One evening, two of my friends and I decided that we wanted to have the whole night free, with nobody checking on us and no curfew. We each told our mothers that we were staying with one of the other girls, so our mothers thought we were staying all night with a friend. We met three young men, and after sizing them up, decided that we could all have some fun together. We drove around for awhile and got acquainted. Finally, we saw what we thought was a park. One couple took a blanket and headed toward a grove of trees; the other couple stayed in the car. The other young man and myself began walking. I know it seems unlikely, but all we did was talk. We talked about life, looked at the stars and discussed his military service; he was home on leave. He was a very nice polite young man.

After awhile we noticed a pair of headlights pull up to the car. So, we headed toward the car to see what was going on. We had parked behind an orphanage. The police had been called, and we walked right up to the police car before we realized it. We were taken to the police station. The couple that had gone into the grove of trees, remained hidden. The guys were both over twenty-one and told the police that they didn't know that we were underage, which was not true. The police for some reason, let the guys take us home, but followed us until they let us out at my place. By this time, it was about 6:00 a.m. We sat on the porch until about 8:00 o'clock and then went in and told Mom that I had decided to come home early.

By this time, I felt pretty sure of myself. I had skipped school, stayed out all night, and considered myself above getting caught, and if I did, I always managed to get out of it. Mom never knew what I was doing, or because of her drinking was unable to care enough to do anything about it.

My period was late one month, and Mom began to scream at me that I was pregnant, calling me a whore and a tramp. I tried to tell her that I couldn't be, because I was still a virgin, but she wouldn't listen. She said that she would get somebody to examine me. But I started before she could get the "somebody" to examine me and nothing more was said about the subject.

I know now, as I look back that somebody was looking after me. The Lord new that someday I would stop running and start reaching out for the love I needed and had given up on. In all the stupid incidents like the previous ones described, and there were more of them, I would only allow myself to go just so far. I know that probably the guys I dated couldn't figure me out. I acted one way, but when it came down to it, I wouldn't put out.

In July of 1956, Emma Mason and Mom decided that maybe a vacation in the country, away from the city and the bad influences would put a stop to my rebellious spirit and the quite obedient child would return.

Romans 8:28 says, "We know that all things work together for good to them that love God, to them who are called according to his purpose." At this time, I had no comprehension of God, or the purpose of my life, but the time would come when I would begin to know and understand my life and Gods purpose in it.

I was sent to Shadow Hill, Mo. to stay with friends of Emma's who also had a son and daughter.

Shadow Hill was a small community. Most were very poor, with no electricity, no indoor plumbing and large families. It was a long way from the city, but one thing that Shadow Hill had in common with the city was the young people looking for a good time. During the first four weeks, I dated three young men all about five to six years older than me. One later became my husband.

Andrew, one of the young men, was always giving me these lines about all the reasons that sex outside of marriage was okay, such as: " Adam and Eve did it; it's normal; and if you really care, you would want to."

I didn't realize at fourteen, that a boy's expectation was quite different from most girls and especially mine. A boy expected a girl to " put out" all I knew was that I felt good because I thought that I was getting the love I so needed, without giving anything back. I didn't realize that I was causing a problem for every boy I dated. Andrew was one that didn't take no for an answer very well. He told the small community that I was easy, so my reputation now was not only hard and tough, but also an easy mark.

I only knew that I could not give myself, until I found somebody that I really loved. I don't know for sure why I felt that way. Maybe, it was a combination of things, the talk Mom gave me when I was nine and the deep conviction that I would never give myself outside of marriage. Also, I knew that if I ever did find somebody that would marry me, there would only be one marriage for me. And at this time in my life, the physical closeness of a man and a woman was not what I was looking for or needed.

A closeness that would make me feel okay, to just be me. Someone that I could identify with, that could understand. This is what I was looking for.

One thing I have learned is to never judge others by one person or experience. The second young man I dated was different. I put him through the same thing, but when I said no or stop that is exactly what he did. I always respected him. Later he married, had a nice family, but died a few years later in a car wreck.

During that month I also met the one that was to become my husband. Once a week at the 66 drive-in was buck night. Everybody that could get on the back of a log truck could get in for one buck. One of these nights a bunch of us kids from Shadow Hill piled onto a log truck, it must have been about nine or ten of us.

On the way to the show a young man that I didn't know, started teasing me like a young man does when he is interested, but too bashful to say so. We sat together on the ground beside the truck and got acquainted during the show. On the way home (back to Shadow Hill) Barry asked me for a kiss. He got his kiss, and we dated a number of times during the remainder of my time there.

We would climb the lookout tower, go for walks along the countryside and just talk. I don't remember much about what we talked about, but I know I felt comfortable with him. Barry would hold me and kiss me, but he never tried to force me to go beyond what I was comfortable with.

After about a month I was to return home, but since I had another month left before school I intended on asking Mom if I could spend a couple more weeks in Shadow Hill.

I rode back to Kansas City with the family I had been staying with. They made frequent trips to the city to see friends and family. This time they were planning to make a round trip, without taking any time to visit. They were going to drop me off at home, I was to ask

Mom about staying a few extra weeks, and then they would pick me up.

I guess Mom had forgot when I was due back home, or was just too drunk to remember. As usual I used my key and opened the door to our apartment. Our apartment was a kitchenette with a bed that folded up into the wall. Mom and a man I had never met were in bed. She looked up at me as if she didn't know who I was. I didn't say a word, walked into the bathroom picked up a few things and walked back out.

I informed the couple I was with that Mom said it was okay. I went back for two more weeks, and spent most of the time with the one man that somehow cared about me. Mom never mentioned the incident, a few weeks later when I came home. I really doubt if she remembered me being there, due to her state of intoxication at the time.

The summer hadn't changed me much, except maybe more dissatisfied with my home life and even more in need of a real home, with a family that could love me.

Between the time I got home and school started I met Richard. Richard was about seventeen years old and a born again Christian. I had never met a born again Christian, or even anybody that was a regular church goer.

I knew I was baptized as a Catholic when I was a baby and occasionally went to Mass. Also, during the time I lived with my grandfather in Minnesota I received confirmation in the church there, but to really know somebody that was serious about God was different. I went to a few Youth for Christ meetings with Richard and began to realize that this was serious stuff to some people. But I wasn't ready to think of God, heaven or hell, at least not yet.

Richard and I would go for walks and talk. One evening he asked me if I would be offended if he kissed me. There were only two other young men that had showed me this kind of respect, and I had left them in Shadow Hill. I gave Richard permission. It was the kind of kiss that let me know that he didn't expect anything more.

As we passed a house one night, on the way downtown to a Youth for Christ meeting, a young man sitting on the front steps said, "Hi" I looked up and it was Barry from Shadow Hill. I said "Hello, what are you doing here?" I introduced him to Richard. Barry said that he was looking for a job.

The next evening, I went for a walk by myself. Just out of curiosity I walked by the house where we had seen Barry the evening before. And just as I hoped he was sitting on the front steps. He asked me who the guy was I was with the night before. I told him it was just a friend.

I met Barry every evening, and Richard at school. Barry would come over to my place and Mom would fix him supper and then we would go to a show or just lay on the sofa and watch television. Late, usually midnight or after we would sit outside in the back of where I lived. We would kiss and hold each other and talk. I don't remember how it came about, but we began to talk about getting married. I was fourteen and Barry was twenty.

Of course, with the late hours we were keeping neither of us was getting much sleep. Barry would leave me about two or three o'clock in the morning, go home, sleep a couple hours, and then go to work. And of course, I had to go to school.

One evening about six o'clock I went over to his sleeping room to wait while he got cleaned up after work so we could go to a show. After he was ready we both sat down on his bed and began to talk. I guess as we talked we kind of relaxed and laid back on the bed, the next thing I remembered was Barry shaking me and telling me that it was five o'clock in the morning.

Barry walked me back to my place scared that Mom had called the police, but I was pretty sure that there was nothing to worry about. The apartment had what was called lattice doors, on the inside, and Mom usually never shut the outside door that opened onto the hallway. Lattice doors had about ten or twelve inch space between the floor and the bottom of the door. I slipped under the door, Mom was in bed asleep, and I whispered to Barry that it was okay.

At school I told Richard that Barry and I were getting married. My relationship with Richard was, I think, a very close personal one, but not like my relationship with Barry. Richard was a very nice, sweet and gentle friend, but I think because of his age, Richard wasn't ready to think about a serious relationship. As young as I was, I wanted a family and for some reason Barry wanted me. I remember Richard taking my hand and telling me that he wanted me to be happy and if Barry could do that, then that was all that mattered. I only saw Richard a couple times after that, and then once after Daniel, our first child, was born.

Since Mom and Cecil divorced, her drinking had continually worsened. Back then all I could see was her drinking. It was as if my real Mom had died and this shell was all that was left. Now as I looked back to those days and know more about Mom from Dad, I understand her better.

To realize that when I was a baby, and all three of us were a family, that Mom was a teetotaler, who went to church and even tried to reform some of Dad's bad habits. Mom hadn't always been the way I knew her, not just the drinking, but the anger and bitterness also that I had sensed, had not always been there.

There were many times Mom would talk of the farm, her family and Dad, but never when she was sober, which was seldom. When she was young, she would climb up into the loft in the barn and daydream of the future. A lot like I did when I would walk the fields and the woods of the farm when I was young. But something happened to her dreams, her faith in God and her zest for life.

I think Mom always regretted letting Dad walk away from her, for she never stopped talking about him, especially as she got older. This daughter also never forgot him.

Over the years I have learned that I can't handle everything by myself. My faith in God is my source of help, my anchor. At one time Mom had that faith in God, but in time she forgot her faith and used alcohol as a way to deal with life.

Mom, when I was a child, would bring every stray cat or dog home she could find and feed it until it would become strong enough to leave. None of us; Dad, Cecil, or myself, ever realized the insecurity and need to know that she was loved. Now years later, thanks to Dad, I remember a lady that cared so deeply but was never able to accept her own self as loveable.

Back to the fall of 1956, after my summer vacation. Barry and I talked about getting married but found out that was all we could do, even with Mom's permission we could not get married, unless I was pregnant, according to authorities. The first weekend of October, after a lot of tears and with Mom's okay, we told the school that we were moving.

Barry was not like a lot of men I knew. He was somewhat of a loner. More than loving each other, we both needed each other. At fourteen years of age, I mistook need for love. But you can't marry and live together for thirty-eight years and not learn to love each other.

We left, Barry and I, Kansas City on Oct. 6 with his sister, Mary and her family for West Palms. We applied for our marriage license and got our blood test.

We told the authorities I was eighteen and no one questioned it.

Barry went back to Kansas City to work. He would be back the next weekend, and we would be married. I stayed with his family that week. It was a week that I have never forgotten. I had never been in this kind of country or with this kind of family. I had always been a loner; afraid I wouldn't be accepted. To cover up my insecurities, I would either pull into my shell and not talk or be so loud and pushy that no one could get close to me. This was one of the times I figured it was best to retreat.

At this time of my life, many years after the events that took place when I was much younger, I have learned to like the person I have become. Thanks to the Lord in my life and recent events, I no longer need someone else to validate me as a person that can be loved as well as love.

I'd been a city kid and here I was by myself and in a house of strangers. Also, I had no brothers, no sisters, no family other than Mom. There was nothing in my life that I could relate this family, of ten siblings, to. The house was full of children and grandchildren. At night all the kids slept five to six in a bed. If there wasn't enough beds, pallets were made on the floor. Which I learned was normal in the country with a big family and lots of company. Kids talking, playing, all at the same time, some fighting as children do.

Barry's family, like most of the families, used kerosene lamps for light, heated with wood in the winter, and meals were cooked on a wood cook stove.

This life was as foreign to me as being in a different country would have been. But my need far outweighed the strangeness. I was going to be married and be part of this large family. Also, I would not have to deal with the problems at home, Mom's drinking and my loneliness. But as the years have taught me you can't run away from your problems, they seem to follow.

That week my emotions alternated between panic, bewilderment, and fascination of what it would be like to become part of this large family.

During that week Barry's Mom and Dad separated and I began to find out that I was not the only one that had problems. If it is true that misery likes company, I learned that you didn't have to look far to find plenty of company.

Barry's oldest brother, Ron and his youngest sister, Wilma, which was one and a half years older than I was, tried to help me feel at home.

On Saturday, October 13, 1956, I became Mrs. Barry Colan. I no longer was Patricia Elizabeth Ryan I finally belonged to somebody. I was a Colan and now I could relate to the name, because there were lots and lots of them. I had not been able to associate my maiden name with myself since I was ten.

We were married at a minister's home. I had no wedding dress, no flowers, none of the usual wedding frills that is considered part of a wedding. However, at last I would have initially, a family. Barry's Mom, Grace, and the minister's wife were our witnesses.

After we were pronounced man and wife, we drove over to the Dairy Princess, had a Maidrite, and a coke. To most people this wasn't much of a wedding. However, to me it was wonderful. At last, I felt warm, protected, such a feeling of completeness and freedom.

By this time Barry's Mom and youngest brother, Chase, were staying with Lou, one of the older girls. Burle, Barry's father, was at the house by himself.

Our Wedding night was spent at the house, with my new father-in-law. The house was empty, compared to the usual gang that was there. We had a bedroom all to ourselves, which turned out to be unnecessary. I had started my period that day, which turned out okay with me. I was in no hurry to consummate my marriage.

Sex was something I didn't understand, in my mind sex had to be connected with love, not just an act that was done because one partner wanted it. I found out that love and sex can be separated, that people don't have to share this deep abiding love in order to participate in the sex act. At the same time, an abiding deep love makes the sex act more meaningful in a marriage. It took many years before I was to finally realize this. We all left the next day; Grace, Wilma,

Mary and her family, Chase, Barry and me, for Kansas City.

We moved into our little one room, third floor walk up apartment, after stopping at Mom's. The first few weeks Grace, Wilma, and Chase lived with us, until Grace and Wilma found a job and an apartment.

During those first few weeks we slept on a twin bed, and Grace, Wilma, and Chase crowded into a double bed. By this time, I had gotten over my period, and my fear of our sexual relationship, our marriage had been consummated.

While Barry's family was staying with us, those first few weeks, one evening we walked over to Mom's. At this time, we didn't own a car, so we walked everywhere. Mom and one of her boyfriends were in the process of breaking open a new bottle of Slow Gin. I did not want Barry to drink, but that didn't stop him. Therefore, to get back at him I took a drink for every drink that he did. Well, it didn't take long, not being used to the stuff, before I was drunk. That was a long night. It was difficult just walking home and Barry didn't help me any. I was dizzy and sick. That twin bed seemed to get smaller, and I kept falling out of it, partly because it kept rocking and partly because Barry kept pushing me off of it.

The first half of that year was great. I didn't think sex was all it was cracked up to be, or at least what I thought it was going to be, but I enjoyed being married. A place of our own, taking care of the little apartment, cleaning and cooking was like a dream. Of course, this dream state I was in did not make my cooking a dream, more like a nightmare. At fourteen I had very little experience in the kitchen. I have to admit, Barry, was very understanding. Hotdogs and hominy were my specialty, partly because I could open a can and partly because I liked hominy. Barry was a country guy and loved beans and cornbread, so how hard was beans and cornbread to cook?

That night when Barry came home from work, I had beans and cornbread on the table, I was feeling pretty proud of myself. Until Barry took his first bite and asked me, "Did you clean these beans? They have rocks in them." Clean beans, never heard of such a thing. Later I took a closer look at the beans that were still in the bag. Well guess what, there were little rocks in them. A lesson well learned, you didn't just dump beans in a pot, like noodles, you looked for the rocks and then rinsed them before cooking.

When our first month anniversary took place, I realized that my period was late, after a few more weeks I figured I better find out if maybe I was pregnant.

I made an appointment to see a doctor at the free neighborhood clinic, since we didn't have any health insurance. As dumb as it sounds now, it didn't dawn on me that a trip to the doctors would include a pelvic exam.

As I entered the clinic, I first noticed that there were a lot of pregnant women there. The receptionist took my name and told me that I'd have to take a seat and when my name was called, I would have to answer some questions before I saw the doctor. About an hour later I was called into a room. They wanted to know my income and if I was married. My family history, parents, siblings and any health problems.

I didn't know anything about my father and very little about Mom. I didn't have any knowledge about my grandparents. I didn't have brothers or sisters. All I knew was that I had missed my period and had been sick to my stomach a lot.

After another hour I was called into a room by a nurse, who handed me this paper gown, I was told to remove all my clothing and put the gown on. After she left I can't explain the feeling, but I would have given anything to have had a mother, a friend, or my husband there, I felt so alone and scared. For the next fifteen minutes I sat there with this paper gown on wondering what would come next.

What I thought was five doctors entered the room, later I found out that only one was a doctor, the others were interns. A nurse was also there. I was told to sit up on the table. I was instructed by the nurse to lay down on the exam table, to slide my buttocks to the end and put my feet in what they called stirrups. By this time, I knew I didn't like this. It was one thing for Barry to see the most private parts of my body and quite another thing for anybody else to see them.

The doctor spread my knees apart and preceded to look me over. Next, he told me to try and relax which I thought was asinine. After inserting an instrument inside me, the doctor had all the interns take a look, explaining that the discoloration showed that I was pregnant and then went on to explain that due to my age it was even more noticeable.

I was carrying a baby, my baby. My child, a part of me that I could love and would love me back. These were feelings I had never experienced before, a sense of completeness. Finally, I had everything I ever wanted.

When I told Barry that evening, he also was very happy, but this was nothing new to him, he already had a family. There was no way he could understand what this meant to me.

We bought a 1950 Plymouth a few months later and could ride instead of walking every place.

My perfect life was soon to become imperfect. My pregnancy was rough. I was horribly sick every morning. Barry lost his job, and we moved in with his mother, sister, and brother.

I cried a lot and began to question Barry's love. No matter what was said, I felt depressed. What had happened to my perfect life? Some may say that due to my age and inexperience, I did not realize that life is not perfect. Even though I tend to agree, I don't believe that it is always a matter of biological age. I have met people of all ages that continue to live in an infallible world. They never have learned to accept the ups and downs as part of life and learn from their failures and their successes.

Barry started receiving his unemployment checks and we moved into .an apartment in the same building that his mother, sister, and brother lived in. Barry had started going out on Friday and Saturday nights with a couple of his cousins. One night he came home sick and drunk, throwing up his entire supper of beans and then passed out. What was left of his supper was in the kitchen sink, he hadn't made it to the bathroom. Like I said, my pregnancy was rough, and I was sick most of the time, but I cleaned the beans out of the sink, gagging as I did.

Another time Barry came home in the afternoon drunk and put his arms around me, wanting to have sex. I pushed him away and he picked up a clock and threw it against the wall, making a hole in the wall and now we had no alarm clock. His Mom and Sister heard the racket and came to see if everything was okay.

Our arguments never lasted long. I would cry and Barry would hold me, and it would be okay. I was so young and needed more than Barry was able to give me. Barry was not raised in a demonstrative family. While they would fight for each other and be there if something was to happen, I never saw them show affection for one another, and that was what I needed.

From the time I knew I was pregnant; I loved this baby. When I began to feel the baby moving around in my stomach, I was in awe with the miracle that was taking place inside of me. We would lay in the bed at night and Barry would lay his hand on my stomach and we would marvel at what we were feeling. I felt such a love and closeness to this little baby. It didn't matter what sex it was. I just wanted it to grow up with a family, and the sense of belonging, love, and closeness

I never had. For my child's sake I would be the kind of mother I never had, and also it would grow up with a father.

Sometime during that first year, before I had my first child, Barry and I took off with Mom and one of her boyfriends to Wichita, Kansas. Supposedly there were jobs to be had, just waiting for us. Barry looked and looked, but there were none to be found, and I was pregnant and fifteen years old, so I couldn't work. I don't know how Mom and her boyfriend got back, but Barry and I sold everything we could and left the rest there and caught a bus back home. Mom turned up a few weeks later.

July 31, 1957, at 6 p.m., I began to feel pain in my back that gradually progressed to my large abdomen. Within a few hours the pain began to get severe. Nothing had prepared me for the experience of childbirth. Grace, Barry's mom, gave birth to all her children at home without a doctor present. During my pregnancy, Grace would tell me of some of her experiences. One of her statements always remained with me, she said that " Birth was like dying."

At midnight, Barry and I headed for the General Hospital, with Grace going with us. I was scared and didn't know what to expect. I was no longer the tough, bleached blonde. Finally, it was 10 a.m. July 31, 1957, I had been placed on the delivery table after a long night. By this time, I was almost hysterical, my water broke, and I remember trying to sit up and being forced back down on the table, at which time I was given an injection via my intravenous tubing. I woke up many hours later back in my room. I realized that I had lost my large stomach. It wasn't long before the nurse came in with a little bundle in her arms and placed it in my arms.

It had been 9 months, 2 weeks and 4 days since Barry and I had married. I had to remember exactly because everybody wanted to know how long we had been married and in the same breath would ask how old my baby was. When the nurse laid Daniel, our son, in my arms the overwhelming feeling of maternal love goes beyond my ability to describe. I had a difficult pregnancy, complicated by my youth and lack of knowledge. We had no money, no job, a very difficult year, but now we had our son, and we were still together.

When Daniel was four months old, I realized I was pregnant again. The love for Daniel and this new one I was carrying made everything bearable. Barry and I never had any money, he was drinking on the weekends, and we were arguing more. As I look back, I know that I made it hard on Barry. I complained a lot about nobody loving me, and the feelings of loneliness returned. That I was plain looking, and not good enough for him. That I was dumb. When I wasn't taking care of Daniel or complaining about my lot in life, I'd be crying.

When Daniel was about five or six months old, Barry and I got into an argument about a disagreement, I'd had with his Mother over how I was cooking. Of course, my feelings were hurt when Grace told me I wasn't cooking the food properly for Barry. I told Grace that it was my home, and my kitchen, and I would cook the way I wanted to. Criticism has always been difficult for me to accept, probably due to my lack of self esteem.

Anyway, Barry told me that I was not to talk to his mother that way. I started crying. I then took Daniel and walked over to Mom's. When she opened the door, I told her about what had happened, and how I had left Barry. She didn't say anything for awhile; then she made a statement, that as harsh as it sounded it saved my marriage. Mom said, " You made your bed, now you'll have to lay in it."

Well due to my pride I could not bring myself to ask Barry to forgive me. So, I decided to feel him out. That evening, I left Daniel with mom and went home. I walked in and told Barry that Daniel had a cold, and I had come back to get the Vicks rub for him. I went straight into the bathroom, closed the door, and started crying. I was so afraid that he wouldn't make the first move. Barry opened the bathroom door and put his arm around me and said, " quit acting so silly. Go get Daniel and get home where you belong." It didn't take long to get Daniel and get back home. Barry, to this day is not demonstrative, but I still know that he loves me, but then, I had too many inner conflicts to realize it.

Mom's drinking was just getting worse and worse, I never knew what man she would be living with next. Also, Mom began making more comments about Dad. A man that she never had anything good to say about when I was a kid, now when she was really drunk, which was most of the time, she would reminisce about him. Most of the time because of the stupor she was in, her comments never made any sense to me, except the words, Mike, or your father.

Barry's sister Mary invited me to church with her one Sunday. I had only been to a Sunday School and church service once, the time I went with a friend, when I was twelve. I had attended a couple Youth for Christ meetings with Richard but sure hadn't been interested in it for myself at the time. As far as churches go, the Catholic Church was the only church I knew anything about. Mom, because of her own personal problems had grown away from it, and therefore, I hadn't really been brought up in it.

I agreed to go with Mary the following Sunday. As we pulled up in front of the church, I realized where

I was. It was the very same church that I had attended that one time, and then I thought they were crazy.

When we; Mary, Daniel and I, walked in and sat down, the congregation began to introduce themselves to me, most of them knew Mary. It was a small Pentecostal church of about thirty-five to forty people. During the congregational singing, I couldn't help but notice how much these people really seemed to enjoy their religion. The look on their faces were of contentment, peace, and happiness. If these people really felt the way they looked, then I wanted to learn more about it.

The minister talked about a personal relationship with Jesus and how he died for anyone of us, even me. This was so new to me, a God that loved me, just the way I was, and would never leave me. At the end of the service an alter call was given, where you personally ask Jesus into your heart. I didn't understand all of it, but maybe, just maybe this was what I was looking for. I made my way down to the altar, knelt and ask Jesus to forgive me, and let me know that I was loved.

I left church and for the first time in my life I knew I had unconditional love. Jesus moved into my life and has stayed with me when at times everybody else I felt would pull away. He is the one that over the years has kept me. There have been times I have pulled away from him, but through those times he has patiently waited for me to return to him. I felt like I had been literally "Born again" on the inside. Nevertheless, I still had the same problems, but now I had somebody to help me with them. For a number of years after finding the Lord to be real in my life, I never felt the sense of loneliness I had felt before.

September 8, 1958, thirteen months after Daniel was born, we had a baby daughter, Anna. This time it was different, giving birth. When labor started, I knew what to expect and I also had a fairly easy pregnancy. I refused pain medications. I was awake and alert when Anna was born. My first daughter, and she was brown eyed too.

When I came home from the hospital with Anna I was met with rejection from Daniel. Grace, Barry's mom, had been staying at the apartment and taking care of Daniel. Daniel, after me being gone for almost a week, didn't remember me. For a thirteen-month-old this wasn't so unusual, but for me at the time I felt that somehow, I just hadn't been a good enough mother. It didn't take long before everything was back to normal, and of course Daniel remembered his mother, but his mother had a problem that seemed to not go away.

We had our problems, never enough money even for the necessities, but oh how I loved my family and the Lord. When Anna was three months old, she developed a diarrhea, that wouldn't go away. She became dehydrated and was placed in the Mercy Hospital. She was there for two weeks. At the same time, I came down with viral Hepatitis, was hospitalized for one month, and Daniel was sick with the big measles. Barry was out of work. Our car was on the blink, so Barry would walk from the city hospital where I was, to the Mercy Hospital where Anna was, almost every day. The hospitals were three to four miles apart. We had a wonderful land lady that worked in a bakery and would give us baked goods. Barry went back to work shortly after I got out of the hospital and things went along okay, at least for a while.

Once before Anna was born, and a few other times over the earlier years, after Anna was born, we would move to Shadow Hill. I learned to wash on a wash board, to use irons that were heated on the wood cook stove. Barry I always knew had a soft spot, he just did his best to never let anybody see it, including me. One morning I made gravy and biscuits on the wood stove. I was still learning. When I served my biscuits and gravy it didn't take long before I realized that the gravy was so thick and lumpy and the biscuits tasted like coal oil (coal oil was used to start the fire), it was inedible. I took off crying, running into the woods. About fifteen minutes later Barry came after me. He told me not to cry, that breakfast was good, which was a lie; I don't think he ever realized how much that statement meant to me.

I learned to build a fire, to read by kerosene lamps and to carry water from the nearby spring. During the winter I learned to really appreciate the Indian summers, when a trip to the outhouse was necessary.

Otherwise, the draft that was experienced when the temperatures fell below freezing made it difficult to concentrate on the task at hand.

We never stayed in Shadow Hill more than just a few months at a time, mostly because I would get so depressed, and cry to go back to the city. One of these times when Anna was a baby, we lived in a old log house about a quarter of a mile off the main road. I remember it with real fondness. Some of the chinking between the logs had long ago fell out, it was winter, and you could watch the snow fall between these cracks. Our furniture consisted of a car seat for a sofa, a couple wooden crates for end tables, a big old wood cookstove, a small wood heating stove, one double sized bed and an old wooden table. We had no electricity and carried water from the nearby spring. We used kerosene lamps for light and lots of homemade quilts at night for cover. Even though it may sound kind of rough, we had fun there, all four of us. But sooner or later, usually sooner, we would have to go back to the city, to find work.

There were a few times, in order to eat and get milk for the kids, that I would go to the Salvation Army and they would give us a grocery order. The Salvation Army would help me in a totally different way, many years later. At this time in my life, a sixteen-year-old mother of two, I couldn't in my wildest dreams see the effect they would have on me thirty-five years later.

A couple years after Anna was born, I began to feel the old lonely feelings coming back. I had stopped going to church, stopped the fellowship with others. Also, I no longer felt the closeness to my Lord, that I once felt. I really don't know how it happened, but I was back to this extreme feeling of isolation, and unlovableness. Daniel and Anna were no longer babies, that I could hold and love. They didn't depend on me like they once did, they were beginning to explore the world around them.

I tried so hard to get Barry to understand my feelings. On the weekends while Barry and his cousins would go out drinking, I'd sit home with the kids and while my love never changed for my family, I still felt so lonely. I didn't want to go out, drinking and living it up. I felt very uncomfortable when I was around a large group of people. I didn't understand my own self. What was wrong with me?

Briana was born January 19, 1962, three and a half years after Anna. Also, my grandfather, Mom's dad died shortly before Briana was born. Barry had to shovel snow in order to get me to the hospital. Briana was also an easy pregnancy and birth. I had someone again to hold in my arms, to feel her little warm body that made my heart feel warm and loved. But Briana was different, so independent. It didn't take long before she was more interested in what was around her, instead of my arms.

We had been married five years when Briana was born. I was nineteen years old. I had by now dropped out of church completely. I was having more and more trouble with my feelings of depression and loneliness. Mom's drinking was getting worse. She would call me and tell me she was dying, I'd either call a cab, or if we had a car that was running, Barry would take me over there. Usually, she would be out of liquor and be very sick. I couldn't buy it, so she would find somebody, anybody, that would go get her a bottle. I'd listen to her talk, sometimes about her Dad, sometimes about mine and a lot of ramblings that I didn't understand. The pain inside of me continued to increase.

Victoria was born October 12, 1965. I was twenty-three years old. I continually needed more and more assurance that I was loved. This new little daughter was another part of that. But I couldn't continue to have babies to satisfy my needs, sooner, or later I would have to face up to my problems. The only thing that kept me from going off the deep end was the children.

One night a couple months after Victoria was born, Barry woke up with a severe headache. Barry's family had a history of migraine type headaches, so we just figured that it was just another sick headache. But as the hours went by it was plain this was different. Barry began to come in and out of consciousness. With the help of two of his cousins, we got him into the car and to the hospital. He was diagnosed with meningitis, an inflammation of the central nervous system, which could be fatal. Barry was released from the hospital after two weeks without any residual effects, except some weakness that would take time to overcome.

Once Barry had recovered, our life went back to the way it was before he got sick. I continued to beg, harp and cry trying to get Barry to prove to me that he loved me. I wanted so much to be held, just to feel his arms around me, but Barry could not hold me without wanting sex. He would use words that would sound so vulgar, and I couldn't respond to him. It got to the point that sex was just a duty to me, I couldn't figure out how to get out of it, so I just gave in.

My depression became so bad that Barry's sister Wilma came down on me hard one day, she told me that I shouldn't be allowed to take care of my kids, that I wasn't a fit mother. I had already decided long ago that I wasn't a good person, and this just seem to verify what I already knew about myself. Barry and Wilma had a big argument with Barry sticking up for me, that should have showed me that he really cared, but I was too far gone to see anything.

I took off walking that day, where I was going, I had no idea. People would pass me on the sidewalk, look at me and then keep on walking. Warm tears ran down my face, but how could I cry when I felt so numb.

I walked for what seemed like hours and finally noticed that I had just passed the Union Station and was on an overpass.

Why was it so hard to get somebody to love me. Love me, not for what they could get out of it or because I expected it or because they felt sorry for me, but just because I was a lovable human being. I wanted so much to stop this pain. The pain was like nothing I have ever experienced. That day I would have given anything to not have been born. About midway over the overpass, I stopped. It was so simple, all I had to do was climb over the guard rails. To just go into oblivion, to not feel, to not have these thoughts that was not only hurting me, but everybody that I loved and cared about.

All of a sudden, I became aware of a loud noise. As I leaned over the guard rail a train was passing below me. There was a man waving at me from the train. Why such a simple gesture stopped me from jumping from that overpass I am not sure, maybe in my state of mind it was as if somebody had finally noticed me. I believe now that the one I turned away from, Jesus, was there trying to reach me all the time. I just had closed my heart so I couldn't hear him.

I turned and walked away from the guard rail. I walked another block and found myself outside the Psychiatric Center of the General Hospital. It was not where I had intended on going, but of course I didn't know where to go, so once again, "He was there all the time." I walked into the hospital; I was still crying and told them I had just contemplated suicide and needed help.

The hospital notified Barry, I don't remember how since we didn't have a phone. After talking with one of the workers and setting up an appointment to start group therapy, Barry took me home.

I spent nine months as a psychiatric outpatient in counseling and group therapy. I met some very wonderful people, including other patients that were as confused as I was. A lot of them had not received help quickly enough and had tried to end their lives, almost making it.

It didn't take long in group therapy and with the help of my therapist before I realized just how much the absence of a father affected my self-image and how I looked at life and people. Especially, how I looked at, or felt about Barry. I had needed a father in my life, and I wanted Barry to fill that need for me. In hindsight, now it is so plain to me. I know it had to have been hard on Barry. When he would put his arms around me, I could never respond to his advances. He would want to make love, while I just wanted to be held and understood. All I wanted was the strong protective arms of my father to close around the little inner girl and pull her close and tell me that he loved me. That I was his little girl.

Mom never realized and Dad never knew of course, how much it hurt this little girl to not have their love. Mom told me that Dad didn't want me, and her bottle told me what was important to her.

The Doctors tried to get Barry to get some counseling, so he would understand, but he refused. As much as it would have helped me for Barry to have some understanding, it was okay. Once I realized why I felt the way I did and let the real pain of rejection surface in a controlled and safe place, where I didn't have to face somebody telling me that the way I felt was "crazy" or "silly", I began to see myself in a different way. I still felt the same loss of a love that I would never know, but at least I wasn't worried so much about being "crazy" anymore and was able to be a better wife and mother. And maybe someday I would really find what I was looking for or at least feel fulfilled.

A year or so later in 1966, or 67, I tried to find my father. I placed an ad in a couple papers; one was in Chicago. I don't know where I got the idea, but I thought that my father was possibly in Illinois. It seemed that when I saw him in 1951 that he had mentioned Illinois, so I thought that was where he probably lived at the time. Twenty-five years later I was to find out how wrong I was. Anyway, it was a large city with a newspaper that had a wide publication coverage. I had two pictures; one took when he and Mom had first gotten married and the other was a picture of him in uniform. I didn't know anything about his family. All I knew was what was on my birth certificate, which gave his name as James Leroy Michael Ryan and that he was twenty-six years old when I was born. Also, it gave his birthplace as Montpelier, Ohio. The ad said, "Anybody that knew the whereabouts of James Leroy Michael Ryan, born in Montpelier, Ohio to contact Patty, " with my address and the next-door neighbors phone number.

One day after work when I came home Barry told me that I had received a phone call from some man in Chicago stating, that he was my father's brother and would call back another time and talk to me. Barry said that he sounded like he was either hiding something, or afraid that I was trying to find him for the wrong reason. Anyway, we never heard from him again.

I finally gave up trying to find him. Mom had told me when I was little that Dad had served time once. Also, that he had only one kidney. I decided that he probably was no longer living.

The loneliness and sense of unfulfillment never left me. I concentrated mainly on the children; they had become my whole life.

Mom came over one evening and of course was so drunk that I just couldn't handle it. I took the bottle, that she always carried, from her purse. It wasn't long before she wanted to know where her purse was. I gave it to her. When she opened it up and found that her bottle was no longer there, she became hysterical and lost control. She was so out of control, that I gave her the bottle back. I didn't understand that you couldn't do that to an alcoholic. Years later, I learned that withdrawal for an alcoholic can be as *psychologically painful, and physically dangerous, as withdrawal* is to a heroin addict.

Mom left, with her bottle, and I don't think she was ever in my house again. However, I was at her place two to three times a week trying to take care of her needs.

Mom remarried for the third time in the early sixties. Dave was twenty years older than Mom. He had money, owned a tavern and a few apartment buildings. I never knew Dave very well, but like Cecil he was not an affectionate man. He was very stern, at least from what I saw of him. Mom by now lived for only one thing, that was how to keep a supply of liquor. What better way than to own your own tavern.

During the years Mom was married to Dave, the kids and I would go over to Mom's place on the weekends. always gone. Dave said Mom always loved to play the piano, and I always enjoyed listening to her play. As a small child, Mom tried to teach me to play, but I was never interested. In the last couple of years, I have wanted to learn to play but now don't have the time to stay with it and practice. Anyway, Mom loved to play the Honky Tonk songs, and it didn't matter what kind of condition she was in; she was always able to play beautifully. I remember "Beautiful brown Eyes", "Honky Tonk Angel" and "A Room of Roses" was among her favorites. She would always fix hot dogs and lasagna for the kids and have me pin curl her hair. Over the years I would ask questions about Dad but never learned any more than I had already been told before I was ten.

1971 started off on a bad note and seemed to continue that way. Dave died January 19, 1971, on Brianas' birthday. Shortly after Dave died, we made one of our many moves to Shadow Hill. Mom married some guy that took a lot of her money. He also destroyed a lot of her mementos; the record that Dad had sent to us when he was in the service, all my baby things that Mom had kept, school papers from when I was in grade school and a picture of me when I was five. Somehow her lawyer got her an annulment.

In June that year, after we had moved to Shadow Hill, one evening, a sister-in-law and I were drinking, I believe slow gin. I became very sick. I had been vomiting over a fence beside the house where we were living at the time. I stumbled onto the porch and found Anna standing to the side in the dark, crying. The next thing I heard I will never forget, also I will never forget how I felt. Anna said, Mom, I'm afraid, I don't want you to be like grandma." My thirteen year old daughter didn't realize it, but it might have been one of the biggest turning points in my life. That was the last time I have ever drunk anything stronger than a soda.

A couple weeks later I was invited to a little country church, that used to double for the one room school that Barry had attended when he was young. I sat there through the service with feelings that I had not felt for a number of years. During the altar call, that still small voice that I had long ago stopped listening to, told me that this was possibly the last chance I might have to make a change in my life and come home again to the Lord. I stepped out from my seat and before I reached the altar, the burdens I had been carrying were lifted. I once again felt that I was not alone. From that day until now he has never left me, and I have never tried to make it again without him. There has been and will be hard times, times of temptation and trials, but always Jesus will remain my Lord and Savior. At times I have cried and cried and have hung on to him and have asked him to hold onto me, but I have always known and felt his closeness. Even when I felt the need to feel the closeness to another human being and the closeness wasn't there, I always felt his love. Being a born again Christian doesn't remove all the mountains, but it does give you somebody to help you climb them, tunnel though them or go around them.

Toward the last of that year, 1971 Mom's lawyer notified me that Mom was in the hospital. I took a bus to Kansas City. Mom was very disoriented and confused, she had been found this way. She had lost weight and had a very blotted appearance. It was plain that Mom was going to end up dying from alcoholism. I tried to have Mom committed to a psychiatric unit to try and get some help for her. One month later Mom had to appear before a judge. She had been in the hospital and of course hadn't had a drink and with medication looked so much better. The judge released her stating that he seen no proof of her needing treatment for alcoholism or committal to an institution.

January of 1972, just a few months after the judge stated that Mom did not have a problem severe enough for long term hospitalization, I was notified again by her lawyer that she was in the hospital. I took off for Kansas City again.

I walked into her hospital room. Mom had no idea who I was, she looked at me, but didn't see me. She didn't talk or seem able to do anything. Her skin had a grayish color to it. Her eyes looked blank, like they were empty. The doctors said that the alcohol content of her blood was so high, that it had literally destroyed a number of brain cells. She might improve but would never be normal again. I wish the judge could have seen her then. For the most part my Mother was gone. Barry used to tease me about not having a father, brothers or sisters and now I didn't have a mother. He told me a few times that I was lucky, I at least didn't have a family to argue with me. He never realized just how much I would have given to have a family like his, of course most people don't realize how much they have.

After Mom had improved enough to be moved, I brought her to West Palms. She remained in a nursing home the rest of her life. I was not allowed to keep her at home. The courts said that because she still had money left and that we were poor and lived without modern facilities, we were not the proper place for her. In time she remembered me, but I was always five or six years old to her. At times, when I went to see her, she would ask," Where's Mike, where's your father" or she would want to see her Dad. Mom had no memory of any of the past except my father, her Dad, and me. Her grandchildren would go see her, she would talk with them but never could remember who they were.

The next few years were good years. We never had any money it seemed, it was always difficult to make ends meet. We remained in Shadow Hill we even managed to buy our own place. It wasn't modern and wasn't what some people would have even considered good enough to live in, but it was ours.

One by one the children got saved and attended church regularly with me. Barry was a different matter, salvation and church attendance was not for him. But I knew down deep there was more going on, than Barry would ever let on.

October 18, 1974, Anna married. She had just turned sixteen the month before. Anna met Jaron at church during the earlier months of the year. When Jaron told us that they wanted to get married, we talked with Anna and Jaron about the decision they had made and how we felt about it being a lifetime commitment. As I am writing this, Anna and Jaron will celebrate their twentieth wedding anniversary this year. They have two wonderful girls. Anna and the girls attended church with me and Anna teaches a Sunday school class. It's not always been easy, but they have made it.

About a year after Anna married in 1975, at church one evening a young girl and her father sang a special. The young girl was our pastor's niece, her name was Diana, and she was twelve years old. Later after church when we were at home Daniel told me that he thought the new girl was sure pretty. I told him that she was too young for him. I'll never forget what he said next "Mom I'm going to marry her. " I kind of laughed to myself, I would never hurt his feelings by telling him that, that was highly unlikely.

Well for the next year Daniel spent every weekend with Diana and her parents. He now had his own car, was trying to finish his last year in school and was also working part time at a sawmill. I worried about him, but I knew I couldn't always protect him and he was such a proud and independent young man.

Sometime in the first couple months of 1977, Diana and her family moved to California. Needless to say, we had one very unhappy son. Every couple days, Daniel would go up to the little country store and call Diana. After a couple months, Daniel quit school with only a couple months to graduation and quit his job. He called Diana and told her father to pick him up at the bus station in Oakland, California.

Daniel joined the army, finished his basic training and asked her parents if they would sign for her to marry, Diana was fourteen at this time. After some counseling with their pastor out there, they were married on May 14, 1977, in Woodland, California. Briana, Victoria and I were present.

Daniel had to leave for Germany where his first tour of duty was. He wasn't able to take Diana with him. A few weeks later we got a letter from him telling us how much he missed Diana. I wrote back and told Daniel that we could get the money for him, so he could send for Diana. We received a letter back from him. I still have that letter along with all the rest of his letters. He said, "Mom, you and Dad raised me and taught me to be responsible, I have a family of my own now and it is my responsibility to take care of my family, somehow I will get the money to send for Diana." He saved every penny he could and a month later he sent her the money, to fly to him in Germany.

July 12, 1978, in Frankfurt, Germany in a army hospital Daniel and Diana's only child was born. A son that they named Joshua Wayne. A month later, with Daniel's help, I flew to Germany to meet my grandson. As I entered the airport terminal, I saw Daniel in his uniform holding little Joshua, with Diana by his side. It was such a beautiful picture, we had no idea what the future would hold. The Lord had given me everything I had asked for. A wonderful son, three lovely daughters and a husband. There wasn't anything else I needed I had everything I needed, in this life.

I spent the next couple weeks enjoying my grandson and basking in the delight I felt as I watched Daniel in uniform, at the base and at home with his family. The memories I have, along with the many pictures, always reminds me of just how much I have been blessed.

After a couple weeks, I was awakened one night when I heard a crash. I jumped up and ran to their bedroom. Daniel was standing, holding onto a chair so tight, that his knuckles were white. Daniel was having severe abdominal pain.

I took Joshua and Diana helped Daniel to the car. As Diana drove the fifteen or twenty miles to the Heidelburg Army hospital I held little Joshua in my arms; wondering what was wrong with his father.

Early the next morning the Doctors told Diana and I that Daniel had Leukemia. They also said that the type he had usually responded well to treatment, but my son was not the average young man.

I walked into Daniel's room; he was laying there staring out the window. Here was a young twenty-one-year-old with everything to live for but would he. He turned toward me and said, "Mom, did they tell you?" I said, "Yes." Then Daniel said, "Do you remember Mom, when I was seventeen and at church, I told you that a voice told me I wouldn't live to be twenty-three." I remembered the incident all to well. Everybody that he told, tried to tell him it was just his imagination. I told him I remembered. He went on "about a year ago I had a dream that something was going to happen, that I would need the Lord to help me."

What do you say, how do you help your son face the possibility of losing everything, especially when you don't know yourself how to face it? I don't remember what I said, I know that we talked, but what I said, or he said is something that only the Lord knows.

The Red-cross notified Diana's parents and Barry and the girls that Daniel was sick, and we would be leaving for the states, as soon as arrangements could be made.

Daniel, Diana and Joshua was sent by Army Hospital Plane from Germany to San Francisco's Presidio Army Base, with final destination being Lettermans Army Hospital for Daniel, and Diana's parents for her.

A seat was obtained for me, with the help of the Red Cross and the Army, on the first plane out for the states. During the trip home, as I flew over the Pacific Ocean I prayed and tried to figure out how I was going to tell Barry and the girls about Daniel, that we might lose him.

Barry and the girls met me at the airport. They were unable to believe that Daniel could actually be seriously sick. The next day Barry and I got on a bus for California. During the next nine months we made seven trips to California. At first, we considered moving to California to be close to Daniel, but Daniel said no, that Missouri was our home and the girls needed us there. Also, he knew his Dad would have a lot of trouble adjusting to the fast pace of life there.

Daniel had nine months of chemotherapy and radiation. He lost all of his hair and was very sick after each round of chemo.

The middle of May 1979, Daniel called, he said, "Mom, the doctors said there is nothing else they can do, I'm not responding to the chemotherapy treatments anymore and they can't give me anymore radiation." The next statement, for an instant, made my heart feel like it would stop. My son said, "I might have two to four weeks left."

Barry and I took the next bus out. Diana's father met us at the bus station in Oakland, California.

The bedroom that Diana had shared with her sisters; she now shared with Daniel. Daniel said that he did not want to die in the hospital, he wanted to be with his family. Their bedroom was at the top of the stairs, just above the living room where Barry and I slept.

On a Wednesday evening June 6, some from the church that Daniel, Diana and Joshua were attending came over. Everybody gathered around Daniel's bed, we sang and prayed.

Quite a few years earlier Daniel asked me once if I really believed that his father would someday give his life to the Lord. I told him then that yes, I believed that someday he would. During the previous nine months Barry had done just that and now, for the first time, he watched with tears in his eyes, as his father knelt with the rest of us and prayed.

June 7, about midnight we heard Daniel call out, "Mom help" Barry and I took the steps two at a time. At the top of the steps, we found Daniel holding onto the wall. He had tried to get to the bathroom and was so weak he couldn't make it. That was the last time we heard him speak. Sometime that night he slipped into a coma.

Barry was the strong one then, especially, after he gave his heart to the Lord. For the first time I had the marriage I always wanted, but I had to lose my son, not forever though, for Daniel said to me during those last few weeks "Mom don't fret for me, I'm okay and I'll see you again someday."

Saturday morning, June 9, 1979, as Diana, Barry and I was sitting by the bed, we heard a sound from Daniel, like a moan or a grunt and in just a few minutes noticed a small amount of blood coming from his nose and ears. It wasn't long before the bleeding became heavier. I couldn't handle it, I knew what was happening, Daniel was beginning to hemorrhage.

Many months earlier I had made a visit to the library and found every piece of information I could on leukemia. Many leukemia sufferers die from hemorrhage, when the blood vessels become so packed with the abnormal cells that they bleed out.

I ran to Diana's parents' bedroom, unable to control the tears. I needed the kind of help that only comes from the one that knew me better than I knew myself. A part of my family and a part of me was about to be taken from this world. I was able to pull myself together after about ten or fifteen minutes and went back to Daniel.

Diana and Barry were sitting beside Daniel, trying to slow the progress of the bleeding by packing his nose and ears. We all agreed that we just couldn't handle this and an ambulance was called.

Within an hour after arrival at the hospital a physician came out and told us that Daniel was gone.

It is strange how we all react at times like this. Earlier I fell apart, and Diana and Barry held it together. Now I tried to comfort everybody else. Diana by this time was out of control, her mom and dad was trying to help her. Barry was softly crying. I asked for a phone and called back home to tell all the family that Daniel was gone. I remember one of Barry's brothers asking if I was okay. I told him I was. Two of Barry's brothers would take off that night with Anna and Victoria, so some of the family would be with us.

Briana was expecting her first child and was advised by her physician to not make the trip from Washington to California. This had hit her pretty hard also and had some experiences related to the death of her brother, that she told me about later on.

Daniel was buried at Woodland, California. After the funeral we hugged Diana and Joshua and cried and came home.

The last of July, Victoria, Barry and I went to Washington to be close to Briana for a while. She was due anytime and having trouble dealing with Daniel's death.

I had been having trouble with depression before we had left Missouri and had been on an antidepressant. It was not getting any better, so I made an appointment with a physician. The doctor stepped out for a few minutes; at which time I decided to see what he had written in my folder. What I read shocked me. He had written that there was nothing wrong with me and in his opinion, I was trying to get a welfare check. I was angry at first, because I couldn't understand how he had come to that conclusion. But it did something for me that I needed.

I left the office, went home and put on some tennis shoes and started walking. Within a couple weeks I was running. When I was running, I felt a sense of accomplishment, a sense of myself. It became a daily part of my life.

The last of July, Anna called, to tell us that she was expecting again. She had already had two miscarriages, so this pregnancy was cause for concern. We planned on returning to Missouri as soon as Briana's baby was born and they were doing okay.

But before Briana's baby was born and we could leave, Barry got a call from home, his father was dead. Barry left for Missouri, while Victoria and I stayed to help Briana. Cindy, Briana's first-born arrived August 10, 1979. A couple weeks after Cindy was born Victoria and I returned to Missouri.

Susie was born on April 12, 1980. Anna had nearly a perfect pregnancy. After the trouble she'd had before, the doctors were amazed how uneventful this pregnancy was. Sometime later Diana told us that was one of the last things that Daniel had wanted. He had told her that he would give anything, to see his sister with a baby, since she had not been able to have one yet. Some of us have always wondered if, maybe, Daniel had put in a special request for a baby, for his sister.

We went back to Washington shortly after Susie was born. I went to work in a laundry and Barry went to work in a woolen mill where Jessie, Briana's husband worked.

Briana had her second daughter, Melina, on June 8, 1981. Jessie accepted the call from God into the ministry shortly after Melina was born.

In the last of 1981 we returned to Missouri again. Victoria stayed in Washington with Jessie and Briana. She had decided that Washington was where she wanted to stay and we always felt that our children, within reason, had to make their own choices. Victoria was sixteen.

We moved to West Palms, just a few houses from Anna and her family.

I began to feel that old loneliness, a sense of unfulfillment. I taught Sunday School, continued to run daily, kept house and helped Barry with his work, but something was lacking. I figured it was "Empty Nest Syndrome" since I didn't have any of the children at home anymore. I felt that there was more that I should be doing.

I went to work at the hospital as a housekeeper in obstetrics. As I would go about my duties, I became fascinated with what was going on around me. The R.N. Supervisor noticed how interested I was in delivery and got permission from a physician and his patient to observe the actual delivery. I stood behind the doctor, with gown and mask on, and watched as a new life was born. The love and joy that I saw on the faces of the mother and father affected me so much, that this housekeeper left the delivery room with tears streaming down her face. How can two people create something that brings such joy and happiness and then someday, maybe, have to give it up? But the joy is so great that even if I had known that I would have to say goodbye to every child I had, it would have still been worth it. But now, I wished I could contribute to the joy and happiness of others.

The R.N. Supervisor, along with two other nurses started telling me, that I could be a nurse too.

How could I, no education, no money and people like me just don't. I would be out of my class. I was forty and every part of my life, including my life with the Lord was governed by what I thought other people felt I should do. I had no confidence in my ability to do anything. I had the Lord, he had helped me and Barry raise and teach Daniel and the girls the right way. He had helped me be a wife and accept that in this life I would not have a son again. But for me to really think that I was capable of being somebody, was foolish. I knew that the Lord loved me and my family didn't say it, but I suppose they loved me, I just couldn't figure out why.

After a lot of persuasion from my nursing friends, I decided to try nursing. Barry was against it from the beginning. He said, I was too old and besides schooling was for the birds anyway.

In 1982, I decided to get my G.E.D. and in a couple months I had my High School Equivalence Diploma. Also, by now all three of the girls had received their High School Equivalence Diplomas. Daniel had received his G.E.D. in the army before getting sick. I studied for a couple months and took the test. I passed with a score well above normal.

Briana had her third and last daughter on November 17, 1982. She called us from the hospital and asked how we would feel about her naming her, after her uncle. We told her that if they wanted to, we would be very proud. Jessica Daneille Barker was named after her father and her uncle. But everybody knows her as Jess. I missed not being there, but with school coming up I could not make it.

October 1983, I started nursing school for practical nursing and Anna had her second daughter,

Ashton on November 11. It was difficult. Barry couldn't see the sense of schooling and with my lack of self-esteem it was a struggle to make it, but in October 1984 I graduated.

February 8, 1985, Mom passed away at the nursing home, where she had lived the past fourteen years. There were only a handful at the funeral. She was buried at the little country cemetery, where most of Barry's family were buried. Mom's only memories, the past fourteen years were of my dad, Mike, her father and me as a child. I couldn't help but wonder, how could she have loved a man that had walked out on her and his child. That was before I knew the whole story.

The next few years were uneventful. I worked as a License Practical Nurse, first on a surgical unit. Then after a year we moved back to Washington.

I went to work in an Army Clinic, it has been the only position that I have really enjoyed in nursing. Barry said that I enjoyed it so much, because the Army reminded me of Daniel, which is possible. We spent another year there. I watched as Briana, Jessie and the girls served the Lord. Jessie was preaching, Briana taught Sunday school and led song service, and Victoria was active in the church as well. Only the Lord could know how very proud of the family He had given me.

We moved back to Missouri. Barry worked in the woods, with timber. We bought a small place in Pomdale, about ten miles from West Palms.

It didn't take long before I had decided to go back to school. I wanted to get my R.N. degree. Of course, Barry couldn't understand why. However, I couldn't blame him, I didn't understand it either.

August 1987, I started college. I had been getting restless and dissatisfied again, with myself. I wanted to work with Cancer patients. I wanted to be an Oncology Nurse.

Barry and I had a lot of trouble over the next three years. It was the same old story, my age and his inability to see any use in education. Also, he was always telling me that I was doing all this because of Daniel.

Which for the most part was true. I probably would not have had the desire to do anything if it hadn't been for him. I believed that everything that happens will produce some kind of a change, it is up to each individual to go one way or another. I could have chosen to sit around and feel sorry for myself. I chose that road once many years ago, I wouldn't do that again with the Lord's help.

My three years in school were difficult. I enjoyed the challenge, and I was on the Dean's list with a 3.50 to a 4.00 G.P.A., during the three years. But I was always scared, I couldn't do it. I was doing it, but never able to accept my own ability. My instructors continually had to encourage me, telling me that my greatest problem was lack of self-confidence. It seemed that I had heard that before.

In 1988, after spring classes, I began to have considerable pain and bleeding. Within just a few weeks I was admitted to the hospital and a complete hysterectomy was done for precancerous lesions. By the last of August I was ready to start classes again.

Then the summer of 89, V... she was getting married August 5 a... any problem with us being able to make... wanted her father to give her away. Which... question, there was nothing that could stand i... of being at our babies wedding. I sat on the front... the church, beside Briana, as I watched are last daughter, with her arm in her fathers' arm, walk down the aisle. Once again it was like a dream come true, but many years ago I knew that dreams do come true, sometimes.

After the wedding and the goodbyes, I dried my tears and we went back home, and me back to my last year in college.

Four months before I was to graduate, I came down with Epstine Barr Virus. It appeared that I probably would not be able to graduate. But by taking it easier I made it.

I graduated May 1990, with an Associate of Science Degree in Nursing. I was voted the most outstanding student by the Nursing Staff. I was one of of the class. I was a Registered Nurse. I was that I had achieved something to be proud of. That I should look at what I had done and where I had come from. However, when I looked in the mirror, I still seen a lonely, fragmented kid of fifty years. Only the Lord and I saw the real me.

I have never been able to work with cancer patients the way I had wanted to, unless we were to leave this area and for a few months we tried to live away from here in Joplin, Missouri. But this was home now for both of us. I loved Washington when we had been out there, but this was Barry's home and now mine. So, I finally took a part time position with a nursing home in June of 1991. I worked, I taught Sunday school, I had long ago given up my running; there just hadn't been any time for it when I started school and now, I wasn't physically able to.

I don't know what started me thinking about finding my father again, but Christmas 1991, I decided to see if at least I could find out about his family. I had decided that he was probably dead, because Mom had told me once that he had one kidney removed when very young due to kidney disease. Plus, I knew that he was between seventy and eighty years old, since I knew he was older than mom.

From my birth certificate I took his name and birthplace as follows; James Leroy Michael Ryan born in Montpelier, Ohio, and sent for a birth certificate. I didn't think much about it, until I received a copy of his birth. For most people it would be hard to understand how I felt, it was just a piece of paper about a man I never knew.

He was named James Leroy Ryan , no Michael. My grandfather was Grover Cleveland. My grandmother was Lena Catherine Basset. My father was born July 12, 1915. My only grandson was also born on July 12. My father if he was still living would be seventy-six years old now. I now had some history, I knew at least where I came from.

I also wrote to the "Leader Interprise" the local newspaper in Montpelier, inquiring about the where abouts of any Ryans in that might still live in the town. I received no replies from the paper or town.

In March 1992, after watching the show "Unsolved Mysteries" I decided to write them and see if they could help me. I received a letter from the show telling me that they couldn't help me but suggesting that I write the "Salvation Army". The Salvation Army had a missing persons Bureau.

I wrote them and received a reply April 1, 1992. They stated that there was a nominal fee of ten dollars, and it would take a couple months, due to their workload, before a search could be started.

I waited not really expecting much anyway. If I could find out just a little bit about the Ryan name, I felt that I would be satisfied.

While waiting to hear, I decided to go down to the local Social Security Office and ask them if I could get any information about my father. I was told that I could write a letter to him and if he was living they would send it to him. In a few days, I went back with the letter. There was a different lady at the desk as I walked in. I told her why I was there and handed her the letter. I asked her if she could let me know when he got the letter. She told me no, I turned to leave, but before I got out the door she was pulling up some information on her computer. The last thing I heard her say was, "He's still living." I sat in the car for a few minutes, until I could stop crying. My father was still living.

Six months later, on October 20, 1992, I was at my night R.N. supervisory position….. It had been 41 years since I had seen or spoke to my father.

I began to cry. Barry asked me if I was okay. I told him I was, it would just take a little time. Barry told me that my father was living in Blue Springs, Missouri. Just three hundred miles away. He gave Barry his phone number and wanted me to call him as soon as I got home, it didn't matter what time it was. Barry also said that he told him that I was a Registered Nurse and he said, "Patty's a nurse, that's wonderful."

When Barry hung up, I sat down at the nurse's station. I was so· shook up that I was having trouble concentrating on the tasks at hand. The staff asked what was wrong. When I told them, one of the other nurses suggested that I call him right away, since I wouldn't be able to think of much else anyway. I called Barry back and told him that I wanted the number that my father left.

In the R.N. office, by myself I shakily dialed the number. I wish I could adequately describe my feelings. I heard the telephone ringing once, then twice, then heard a female voice say "Hello." I said, "is James Ryan there." She said, "Dad, I think it is Patty."

Nothing in my life had caused me this much anxiety, or apprehension. Was this woman I heard my half sister? What would he sound like? Or worse, what would he think of me?

I heard some one pick up the phone, without saying anything. It seemed like a lot longer than it really was, but finally I heard him say "Hello." I started to cry, again! Then he said, "Patty." I said, "yes." Then I heard him sob and say, "Are you okay." I told him I was and that I was just so shocked, I didn't know what to say. We both were crying so much that a conversation was difficult. He asked me about mom, I told him that she had died in 1985. It took him a few minutes before he could say anything else. I told him that I was calling from work, and it was difficult for me to talk, but that I couldn't wait until I got home. I told him what time I'd be leaving work, and he said, he would call me when I got home.

The next couple hours were strange. I worked, doing what I usually did every evening, but it was as if there were two of me. One a nurse taking care of my patients and the other one wondering about what all this would bring about. What did he look like? What would it be like to actually meet my father? Where had he been all my life? There were many more questions in my mind, but enough was enough, I was too overwhelmed to think anymore.

As I opened the door with my key, I heard the telephone ring. It had just been a couple hours since I had called Dad, but it still seemed like a dream. I picked up the telephone. Dad said, "Patty." I said, "yes." I told him a little about the girls. Also, about Daniel, to which he said, "Oh god." I told him how much I would like to see him, he said that he would like to see me also. I asked him, who answered the telephone earlier. He said it was his wife, Loran. He also said that I had met her many years ago, and had also met his stepson, William.

It was so difficult for either one of us to talk, because of the emotional feelings that we were both caught up in. Dad stated that he would write me, and I told him that I would also write him. When we hung up I said, "Goodbye, Dad." it was a wonderful feeling, but also strange to be telling my Dad bye.

To tell all my feelings that went on in those first few days, and everything that was said would take more time, and paper than what I want to go into at this time. But I called each one of the girls and Diana in the middle of the night to tell them. I spent most of the night going through old pictures, a couple that mom had of dad when they were both young.

I mailed a letter to Dad the next morning and waited.

Monday morning, I couldn't wait for the mail to run. Sure enough, there was this letter addressed to Patricia Colan with a return address from Mike Ryan. Just to see that name, the name now with a face, made it all seem more real. The following is an excerpt from that letter;

"Dearest Patricia,

Yesterday I received the most pleasant surprise, and might say shock of all my seventy seven years…

I am as much, or more to blame for your mother and myself parting. I went into the army and was there for thirty-three months. I had an alternative motive for wanting to get into the service, that I will tell you some day if you would like to hear it. That was in April 1943. I know I should not have left you and your mother alone, and for that I'm sorry.

I am sending you two pictures, but I want the one back that is of you when you were a baby. I think your mother sent it to me when I was in the army.

I LOVE YOU PATTY

Your Dad"

"Dad" it was such a strange feeling to say it and realize it was my Dad. To finally put a real live person to my imaginary father. Almost fifty-one years old and find my father. If I live to be a hundred, I'll never stop being amazed and in wonderment at how life can turn about face, when you least expect it.

We spoke two or three times with in the first four or five days. Always at midnight. I had always enjoyed the midnight hours, now I knew why, my father had also. Wednesday evening, I talked with Barry about me going to see my father. He was not too happy about me taking off, but I had always been pretty stubborn, so I made plans to drive to Blue Springs the following Saturday.

I called Dad and told him that I was coming up Saturday morning. The telephone is not the best way to get to know somebody, even more so when it is a father and daughter. So, we were both very apprehensive. Loran, Dad's wife, told me that she was also looking forward to seeing me.

Thursday night I wrote in my journal; "Well, it's been four nights since I first heard my father in forty years speak to me and day after tomorrow, I'll see him. I don't think I can put in words how I feel. It's one of the strongest emotions I've ever felt. It's strange, but I feel somehow, complete. I have not had that feeling of being worthless, dumb or ugly at all this week."

Saturday morning, four o-clock I was up. I made breakfast and took a shower. I've never been a person that had to have every hair in place and dressed just so. But this morning was different. I couldn't help but worry a little about what my father would think of me. I wondered did he go to church, was he a Christian, what did he like and dislike?

Barry kept asking me if I was okay. He said, "You are not going to take off if your nervous and crying. " I kept busy getting ready and told Barry that I was okay.

It was five when I pulled away from the house. My last words to Barry was "don't worry, I'm okay." I stopped at the end of our street, before pulling on to the highway, and cried. I couldn't let Barry know how scared and nervous I was. He had never understood my feelings about my father and myself.

During the five hour drive, I cried a number of times, but the Lord was with me. I got in Blue Springs about ten a.m. I couldn't bring myself to follow the directions and go straight to his house. I passed a Walmart store and decided to stop and get a present for Dad and Loran. I walked around for fifteen minutes, or so. I couldn't find anything that I felt would be appropriate, so I called their house. Loran answered, I told her where I was and that I wanted to get Dad something. She said, that he didn't need anything, but I said that wasn't the idea that he needed something, I needed, to get him something. She still couldn't help me, so I told her that I would be there in just a little bit. Finally, I picked out a key chain and had it engraved with "Dad, Love Patty." I picked out a ceramic carousel for Loran. They were not expensive gifts, just a little something to show them how I felt. Of course, there was nobody that could know how I felt.

I found the house. It was a nice house and new, nothing like I had ever lived in, which just made me more nervous. I followed the walk around to the door and rang the doorbell.

Never, never in my life was I more nervous and scared. I almost turned and left, but just then the door opened. "Oh Patty, you haven't changed. I remember the last time I seen you, you were just a little girl." With that Loran reached out and put her arms around me at the same time stating "Come in."

Just inside the door, standing in their front room with Loran's arms around me, I saw what I had come three hundred miles and forty-one years to see, my father.

A large man, with thin, gray hair well over two hundred pounds and over six feet tall was pushing himself up to a standing position, from his wheelchair. I turned from Loran, toward my father. As I crossed the five or six feet to him, he said, "Patty" I said, "Don't Dad" he was having difficulty standing up. He sat back down. I put my arms around him, as I felt his arms around me.

After, I don't know how long, I pulled back and saw something that will always evoke tears and wonderful memories. I was looking back into the same brown eyes that my mother saw, when she looked at my father and me, all those many years ago. Also, I saw tears and love for his daughter.

I sat in a chair a few feet from dad's wheelchair, and we talked for ten or fifteen minutes. For the first few minutes it was difficult, but there was something, a bond that transcended the years, that we both felt very strongly.

Dad had peripheral neuropathy and a laminectomy of the cervical vertebra which left his neck in a position, which made it impossible for him to raise it above a certain 80 position. Because of this Dad transferred to his recliner, which he also slept in.

It seemed natural to sit on the floor next to his chair. It made it easier to talk, because of the fixed position of his head and neck, and at the same time it was more intimate.

During the next fifteen hours we talked about two lifetimes, his and mine. We both cried many times that day and at times we still do, especially when we got to talking about Mom.

We talked about so much that now it's hard to write about it, just exactly as it took place. A lot of what I had to tell him I know was hard on him. But I had spent my earlier years alone trying to understand as a child, what had happened and what part I played in it and why my father had not been there for me. Even though, with Gods help, I had grown up and raised a family, I needed my father now to understand what it had met to me for him not to been there. So, we spent the next hours finding out just what the years had met to both of us.

I told Dad about Mom's drinking. The men in her life, after him. The years in the nursing home, and how she died from cancer. I felt his large hand, as it held mine and saw his tears slide down his face as I talked about Mom. He looked at me when I told him about her life and said, "Oh God, no not your mother." He told me that he had never seen her take a drink or smoke a cigarette. That she would tell him that he should never take God's name in vain.

Many months later, after this first meeting, it was evident that over the years he had forgotten the importance of God's name.

Dad related how he and mom separated, which I told at the beginning of my story. Also, how after seeing me a few times when he remarried, he had decided to go on with his life, since it was plain to him that Mom and I were no longer apart of his life. He didn't say it, but I remembered that he had a stepson, which I think helped take the place of the daughter he had.

The only time Dad left his chair, and I left his side was to eat that day.

We talked about that day, when I was ten. Our memories of that day told both of us that we had never forgotten each other. I was a child afraid to reach out to him. He was a father that had gotten so use to walking away, that it was the only thing he knew to do.

I found out that Dad and Loran had spent eighteen years in Florida. They had moved back to Missouri in 1975, and 1979 he became disabled. When I was ten and thought that Dad lived in some other state, he had lived just a few hundred miles from me in Blue Springs, until 1955. They left and went north and then south to Florida. The year before Daniel died they moved back to Blue Springs. In fact, Dad said that he stopped in West Palms at a motel before going on to Blue Springs, never realizing that he had a daughter and four grandchildren living there.

Dad has never felt the presence of the Lord. He does not know, if there is a God or not. He was somewhat I think, at first, disappointed that I didn't drink and party. He had never been exposed to the Christian life, not since Mom anyway.

But as we talked and talked, we were amazed at how much our personalities were alike. We both like to read. We both have this insatiable curiosity, always wanting to see what is around the next bend. This is what Dad said made him enjoy bumming around the country when he was young. We both have very strong opinions and tend to find it very difficult to give into another. Even with each other we are both sure that we are right. Of course, this does help us to understand each other, if either one of us has a different viewpoint, we realize that the other is not going to change. That is unless the other can prove their viewpoint. We both love being showed that we are loved and we both love showing each other. Dad said that him and Mom had a very loving marriage, until he left for the army.

Dad learned about his grandchildren and my life. He told me that he was so sorry for all the years. That if there was a God, that he thanked him for me and my desire to find him. He said, he wished he would have been there for me, but that what ever time he had left he would always be here for me now. Again, I wish I could describe the closeness we felt. I've had people ask me, how could I feel like he was my dad. I don't know, I just know that he was, and the bond was there.

Loran stayed in the dining room, working on crossword puzzles and reading. Occasionally, she would ask Dad a question concerning the puzzle she was working on. Dad said, that was her pass time, so I never thought anything about her not talking or setting in the living room with us. I also, figured she was giving us time to get acquainted.

About five that evening William and his wife came over to meet me. William said, he remembered me when I was about five. Dad showed me a picture of William and me. We were standing on a step with William's arm around me, like a big brother, I guess.

It looks like a four and a half, or five-year-old would remember things like that. I remembered being in kindergarten when I was five. Why didn't I remember something as important as my father and a stepfamily?

It was two o'clock in the morning when we quit talking. Dad always slept in his chair; he had for the last thirteen years. Loran had said earlier, that when I got ready for bed I could sleep in the other twin bed in her bedroom. So, finally Dad and I said goodnight, with Dad giving me a hug and kiss, along with a few tears.

Sleep was almost impossible, I continued to cry into the pillow, trying to muffle the sounds. We had talked about so much. It was so emotionally exhausting to look at my father and remember the year I turned ten, the times I wanted him so much and now he was here in front of me. Also, to watch him cry with great shaking sobs, as I told him of Mom's life and how she finally in the last years of her life only remembered her Dad, her Mike and Patty.

On the second day, after breakfast Dad said he wanted to take me for a ride. So, he wheeled himself out to the garage and by setting on the rear bumper, he was able to lift his wheelchair into the trunk of his 68 Buick. He then made it to the drivers seat by holding onto the car and climbed in. It was really something indescribable to set there by my father as he drove me around. He took me over by the lake where they had lived when I was ten. There he introduced me to a old friend of his, telling him that I was his daughter.

Next, he took off going toward Kansas City, which was about twenty miles from Blue Springs. Dad showed me where they had lived the few times that I had seen him after the separation. It was also where the picture of me and William was taken. We drove down the street where I had once lived with Mom and my stepfather, and the place that I had seen Dad.

So many of the places, of the past were gone. Freeways, overpasses and some vacant lots had taken the place of some of my childhood memories. Progress may scrape the material remnants of our memories, but it can't rob us of the internal memories. They will always be there just inside waiting to come foreword. I didn't know it then, but the next weeks and months would prove to be even more enlightening.

Dad had one last place he wanted to show me. He drove downtown and right in the middle of traffic he stopped at 1017 Locust. I looked out the window. Dad said, "Have you got your camera." I told him "yes." He said, "see that building." I said, "yes." Next, he pointed out the window and said, "That window up there on the corner, on the second floor was your first home. This is where I worked, and we lived when you were born."

The building was old, but you could see a few people in the lobby. On the front of it you could still make out the words, Schuyler hotel. It and one other old building were in the middle of the rebuilding of the downtown area, most of the old places had been torn down. I took a number of pictures and Dad started back to Blue Springs. During the drive back dad continued to tell me of the days when we lived at the Schuyler and how happy they were then.

After three days of this it was time for me to leave, but I didn't want to and dad didn't want me to either, so I called my place of employment and Barry, asking them if it was okay for me to be gone a couple more days.

The nursing home said they could get along a few more days without me, but I could tell that Barry wasn't very happy with me staying a couple more days.

I stayed two more days. I left about eleven o'clock in the morning with dad setting in his wheel chair in the garage, crying. Again, I had to stop before pulling into traffic to get control of myself. The last thing we said to each other was that we would write and see each other again in a month or so. We wrote each other often over the next couple weeks.

Excerpts taken from dad's letters;

"Oct. 31, 1992`

Saturday

My Wonderful Darling Daughter,

It is exactly eleven hours (since I had left that morning) 8:30 Saturday evening, and I am trying to watch Beaches, on T.V. and write you at the same time. Is that the movie you told me about?..... I was going to wait until Monday to write, but I couldn't wait. Only five days can't make up for forty one years….. I love you so much and miss you….. I don't ever want to lose you again….. Thank Anna and Ashton and Susie for the note they sent me. I would like to meet all of your family sometime and maybe I will…..

With all my love, Dad"

"Nov. 3, 1992

My Dearest Daughter,

I love saying that, or writing it. I must be the happiest Dad, or at least one of them. I love you so much, Patty and I think about you all the time. Don't ever stop missing me, because I can't stop missing you…..

I would like to have the address of all of your children….. All my Love and prayers to you.

Dad"

The letters I wrote I signed "Love and Prayers."
"Wed. Nov. 4, 1992

Dear Daughter Patty,

….. I feel like my life has been worth something after 72 years. You are my daughter and I love you as no one else could. Some people don't like to be called endearing names, but I feel like I am not expressing myself to my full feelings if I don't use some endearing words. You feel special because you are special. You will never feel lonely again, as long as I am around. You are not a small child anymore, but I will always remember you as that little 10 year old I met so many years ago….. Just a couple weeks ago I never thought I would ever have a daughter, or a Patty…..

Sleep good Sweetheart. I love you.

Friday afternoon"

(Dad wrote about his life and years in Florida)

"This afternoon I sealed my letter to you and was going to mail it in the morning, but I will answer your small letter of 9 pages. Don't worry about writing too much, I love the long letters. I am happy finding me has made a difference in your life, but please don't let it come between, or affect any of the other people you love! If it does that it will not make finding me wonderful as it does now, for both of us. Yes! I wish I had been there for all your previous life, but what we have now is so rare that I am happy beyond all my expectations….

(Dad wrote about his years in the South Pacific, during the war)

…..Patty, your mother couldn't help what she did, and she always loved you and once loved me too.

All my love,

Dad, It just tickles me to sign my name like that.

P. S. I am trying to get my Baptismal Certificate and a copy of the wedding certificate that Father Murphy performed with your mother and me….. could you try to get a copy of the wedding certificate from Minneapolis, Minn. of your mother and me. It was by a justice of the peace. I don't know where to start.

love Dad"

"Sat. night November 9, 1992

1:30 A.M.

I'm in my chair again, just came from the den, where I wrote a few lines to Victoria . She called me about 4:00 P.M., this afternoon. We didn't have a very good connection, but I am so glad she called. I got a big kick when I told her that Daniel looked so much like me, that both of us squinted when we smiled. (I gave Dad an army picture of Daniel, and they did look a lot alike, when comparing Dad's army pictures with Daniel's. She laughed and said so does her eyes….

I think it would be great if you could come, so we could be together on your birthday. I was with you on only one of your birthdays, your first one.

Sunday night. 8:45, in 3 hrs. and 45 minutes. I'll be talking to you….. I wrote only a few lines to Victoria, in hopes she will write and tell me all about her life and her husband…..

5:18 Mon. morning, and I can't go back to sleep, so I will try to write a few more lines…. I hope to see you on the 14th. (November) I run out of something to write about, but I could say I love you so many times to fill this page, but I don't think that would be news to you….. The letter I wrote to Victoria I noticed that I wrote some words with all capital letters, ….. so help me I didn't know that I had the capital key down …..

Love you my Patty
Dad"
"Monday night, Nov. 10, 1992

I didn't get a letter from you today, and I miss it so much. I go to the mail box every day, and no mail from my daughter today…..

It would be just great if you could come this Saturday, and to be with you on your birthday would be the biggest thrill of my life…. the only one we had together, you don't remember….

With love

Dad"

It had been almost three weeks since I had seen Dad. Even with all the letters and talks on the phone at night, when I would get off work, I still couldn't hardly wait to see him again. I would read his letters over and over, still finding it hard to believe. My letters to him were a lot like his, telling him how much I loved him.

Barry and quite a few of my family and friends found it hard to understand why I felt so strongly about a "stranger." Even my pastor at the time was amazed that I felt no bitterness, because of Dad not trying to find me over the years.

Early that Saturday, I took off again to see Dad. I was a lot better this time, at least I didn't have to pull off the road to cry, but I was still so excited to see him and was having trouble accepting this new life. I guess I had never over the years, been able to imagine what it would be like to have a father. I would catch myself wondering if this is what it was like to have a father, but I knew this was different from what others felt about their father. Here I was fifty-one years old, with a seventy-seven-year-old father. But I felt like a child. A child that was afraid to let their father get out of their site. And when I looked at Dad, I could see that he was not a young man, but I felt deep inside of me that I was ten and he was thirty-six.

I arrived at Dad's about noon. Dad gave me a big hug. Loran said, "Hi Patty. " Dad told me how much he had missed me, and I took the place that had become mine, on the floor beside Dad's chair. As before we talked and talked, it seemed that we would never run out of anything to say to each other. I was finding out just what Mom had always meant, when she told me, "Your just like your father."

I had always been fascinated with life and what made people and things tick, always wanting to know what was around the next bend. Dad told me about his hobo days and all the people he met. He had also, twelve or thirteen years earlier started writing a book about his life, and in the previous three weeks had been reading my journal that I had left him with him previously.

Both of us enjoyed reading, chocolate, good movies (what was good was a matter of opinion), and a number of other things, plus we were both very set in what we believed to be right and proper, which in time would cause us some problems.

Late that evening, all three of us were in the kitchen getting ready to eat, when Loran turned to me and said, "Patty, I'm going to lay my cards on the table." Before she could say anything more Dad said, "I think you better pick them back up." The tone in her voice was flat and matter of fact. The tone in Dad's voice was anything but matter of fact, I knew something was wrong.

Loran said, "I don't want you coming back up here, every two or three weeks is too much. I'm not up to doing any entertaining. You can come up and see your Dad some place else. I think a few hours every two or three months is enough anyway."

Dad didn't say anything just gave me a look that said, we'll talk about it later and wheeled his wheelchair toward the bathroom. After he was out of the room Loran said, "Your Father is not what you think he is." Then went on to tell me that he was a liar, that he had lied to her about his age and in general wasn't much of anything, at least to her.

I just sat there too stunned and confused and also embarrassed, to say anything. I had a hard time fighting back the tears. I wasn't about to let her see that she had got to me. The next couple hours were strained, I thought about leaving right then, instead of waiting until morning as I had planned, but Dad kept patting my hand and whispering that it would be okay.

After Loran went to bed we talked, but not about what happened. I couldn't help cry, why did she treat me this way when she acted so happy to see me on that first visit? Dad asked me to be patient, that things would change. It was difficult that night, trying to sleep in the same room with Loran knowing that she didn't want me there.

The next morning about eight I left, again with Dad sitting in his wheelchair crying. I was also crying which worried Dad. He kept telling me to not cry, because he was afraid I would have a wreck. As we hug and said goodbye, he again said it would be okay and I was to call him as soon as I got home.

This was crazy, all the way home I cried and wondered if I would see Dad again.

When I got home and told Barry what happened he was upset. He said I wasn't going back and be treated that way. That week was so difficult. I asked the church to pray about the situation and waited. I got two letters that week from Dad. An excerpt from one of them as follows.

" Dearest Daughter Patty

…..Patty give me until the first of January and there will be some changes made….. Since you came into my life, I have been so much changed that people around me here should be happy. When anything would go wrong I would use this nasty word all the time (S---) and cuss a lot. I can understand why someone would tell you that I am not what I seem to be. Who knows I might turned out to be human after all…..I feel so much better and am not mad at the world anymore…..

With all the love that's in my heart.

Your Dad"

The following Friday, I got a call from William. He said, "Patty, Dad wants you to call him at twelve tonight. " I asked him if everything was okay, he said, "just call him tonight. "

I didn't know what to expect. Dad answered, I asked him if he was okay. He said, "do you still want your old Dad. " I told him, "of course I do. " He said, " I'll see you tomorrow, when I get there. " I started to question him, but he just said that he would tell me everything when he saw me.

Needless to say I was scared and felt a sense of alarm, at the idea that he was going to take off by himself. He couldn't walk without something to steady him, and then not more than a few feet. It was very difficult for him to hold his head up for a prolonged period, due to the neck surgery he'd had. And he was going to drive three hundred miles, what if something happened to the car?

I didn't sleep much that night and all the next day I kept imagining horrible things, a heart attack, a wreck, or his car broke down and no one to help him. He was supposed to leave at six a.m. It was two p.m. and he still wasn't here, so I called William. His wife answered the phone, and I burst out bawling. After I told her why I was so upset she said that William wasn't there, but she would get a hold of him and have him call me back. About fifteen minutes later William called, He said that he tried to talk him out of leaving, but when he got something in his mind there was no changing it. He also said that Dad had plenty of money, for me not to worry, he would be okay.

About five o'clock his old blue 68 Buick pulled in, with Dad all smiles. I was so relieved to see that he was okay. Barry and I helped him out of the car. Dad and Barry shook hands as I introduced Father-in-law to Son-in-law. I pushed Dad up the ramp, that Barry had made earlier and into my house.

I was so proud to have my father in my home and also, so proud for him to meet my family and the family he never new. Anna, Jaron and the girls came over to meet Grandpa and Great-grandpa. Anna and Dad took to each other right away.

Dad asked us if it was okay, until he could get a place of his own, to stay with us. I told him that we would love it. He wanted to know how Barry felt about him being there. told him that it was okay with him also. Barry and I had talked about it and he told me that it was okay.

You have to remember Barry had never been much of a joiner. He preferred to just let things and people alone and go about his own business. By this time Barry had a small tire repair shop in the garage, and he spent a great deal of his time out there.

That night Dad told me what happened. He and Loran had gotten in an argument (He didn't give me all the specifics, but I got the idea it was about me and Mom). He said that Loran had made a derogative statement about Mom, in the heat of the argument. He told her that she didn't know anything about Lettie, since she had never met her. With that Loran said, "That's what you think, I did meet her once." Dad had never known that Mom and Loran had met, until then. Dad said that he told Loran that if I wasn't welcome then he wasn't either. She told him that she would help him pack. That evening, Dad went to Willam and borrowed five hundred dollars. Then put his clothes, with William's help, into the car the next morning and left.

Dad stayed with us for three weeks. We spent night after night talking and learning about each other. He was so kind, so loving and tender. I never heard an unkind word, or a cuss word from him. He talked about Mom, and how much he loved her now. He wanted to be buried beside her. He said if there was a God, then God would let him see her again. He wanted to tell Mom that he was sorry he left us, that he should have tried to work it out with her, instead of giving up so easily.

I was spending four and five hours a day with Dad. Barry began to resent the time I spent with Dad. He told me that I was forgetting my family. He asked if I thought about how the girls felt, about my being so wrapped up in my Father. He said that nobody could feel the love that I said I felt for a man that was a stranger. My home life was getting more strained. But Dad was there anytime I needed his hand to hold, always telling me how special I was. I had never had anybody to make me feel so special until now and I was soaking up all of it I could.

After a couple months of Barry and others in the family telling me that it was time to pull back, I called a counselor, that specialized in this sort of thing. I talked to her about how my family felt and that I felt I had to be with Dad every day. The idea of not seeing him would make me cry. She told me that as long as the separation from my Father had been, it was not unusual for me to feel this way and a few months had not been long enough for me to feel secure yet. I tried to not worry about it. Anna helped by telling me that she understood.

Dad was hospitalized for a week in January for pneumonia and I got to where, after he got out of the hospital, I was afraid that I would find him dead someday.

In April, Dad was served with divorce papers. A month later at the age of seventy-six, my father was single again, after forty-six years of marriage. By this time, I'd learned a lot more about his life over the years.

About this time, he began to have, what we later realized, were panic or anxiety attacks. Through the daytime he was okay, but as it got later he would begin to feel like he was locked up. He would begin to swear, get sweaty, his heartbeat would start beating rapidly, he would be afraid to go to sleep because he knew that he wouldn't wake up. Finally, I got him to go to the doctor and was given an anti-anxiety medication. The spells got better, but did not go away entirely. From that time on he began to swear more and talk as if he hated the whole world, except, he said Anna, Barry and myself.

Dad told me that about 1986, they got into it and he left and went to Florida but returned in a week. Before Loran would let Dad stay, Dad had to sign his share of their home over to her and he kept the 68 Buick. He said that when I found him, he sure needed me. Dad talked with a friend of his and Lorans a few months after the divorce, and according to this friend, Loran was afraid that if Dad was to die, I could make a claim on his share of the home. A divorce made their arrangement legal. I have trouble understanding how anybody could be so suspicious of others.

By June 1993, the last eight months was beginning to take a toll on me. Dad seemed to need me with him all the time, and when I was with him, I would try to think ahead how would I handle Barry at home. Barry was not pleased with the time I was spending with Dad, and when I was home, I was worried about how Dad was. I was working three days a week. Trying to study for my Sunday Class work, which I took very serious. Plus, trying to keep up with all the other things in life. It didn't help that I had always worried about making sure that I didn't upset anybody. I tried to take a leave of absence, but I was told that was impossible, so I quit my job.

A week later I couldn't take any more. I had repeatedly asked Barry if we could make a trip to Minnesota, a place that I had always wanted to go back to, almost like going home. Barry's answer was always, there's no sense in it, that I hadn't been there since I was a kid so why in the world would I want to go back. I wrote a letter to Dad telling him I had to get away for awhile and tried to explain why. I wrote a letter to Barry, also trying to explain how I felt. I also told him that I wouldn't be coming back to him. I had given up trying to get him to understand. I told neither one where I was going. I called a Home Nursing Service and gave them Dad's address and Doctor's name. I told Anna that I was leaving, and that I would be back home or at least back to West Palms in a week or so, and would she check on her Grandpa for me.

I knew that if Barry knew what I was going to do there would be a fight and I just couldn't face it. So, the day before I left I packed my clothes. I didn't have any cash so with a credit card I bought a bus ticket, called a car rental service in Minneapolis, Minnesota and reserved a car, I also had a room reserved in St. Cloud, Minnesota. After Barry went to sleep. I left my letter, that also told him that the car would be in West Palms, parked in the lot where Dad lived, and drove to town. I left Dad's letter with him, after I stopped to check on him, and took a cab to the bus station to catch the eleven o'clock bus going north.

    As I sat in my seat and watched the familiar scenes go by, I felt that this trip would reveal some new aspects of my life. What they would be, I didn't know. The bus pulled into Kansas City, Mo, at six a.m. I had eight hours before the bus would leave, for Minneapolis, Minnesota. I rented a car for the day, and took a trip back to earlier days, to the neighborhood where I grew up. It's hard to describe how I was feeling. As I walked through the school I attended in Junior High, and along the streets and sidewalks I played on, taking pictures of park I played in, I felt that I was myself. I wasn't having to be a wife, a mother, a daughter or a nurse, I was just being me. Many of the old places were condemned, the building that Emma Mason owned, where we had lived for a number of years was boarded up. Memories flooded back with such a bittersweet feeling.

I drove over to what used to be the union station and where the overpass was. There was a park near by that overlooked the whole area, I stood there and looked at the union station where Dad had left us for the army, and at the overpass thinking of that day when I had considered ending my life, and thanked God that he had stopped me. I drove over the Schuyler Hotel, I was going to go in and see if it was possible to take a look at that second floor, front apartment, my first home. Sadly, I found it boarded up, it had been condemned since Dad had brought me to see it, a short eight months ago. Finally, it was time to take the rental car back and catch the bus onto Minneapolis.

Dad had talked so much about Minneapolis, and the time, him and Mom had spent there, that I felt I knew it by heart. The bus arrived in Minneapolis around six a.m. and the car rental didn't open till eight, so since the bus station was downtown, I decided to take a look around. I found a small map of the downtown area and sure enough just eight blocks away was Hennipin and Nicollete Avenues.

I walked down Hennipin until I came to the Gateway and then followed Washington a block to Nicollete. All the old buildings were gone, that Dad had told me about, but the general layout of the streets were the same. The car rental agency was in the downtown area, so I walked over there, got my car, went back to the station and picked up my luggage.

It had been about forty years since I had been in Minnesota, but my memories were good and with a map I had no difficulty finding my way. It was strange, here I was fifty-two and the first time I was really on my own and it felt good. Oh there were moments that I would catch myself thinking about Barry, Dad and the girls, but I needed this and for a change I was going to find out about me. It was so nice, as I drove along enjoying the Minnesota countryside, that I had enjoyed so much as a child. I also was liking the feeling of driving a new Pontiac Grand Am, that I had rented. As silly as it sounds, I felt like a young woman, away from home for the first time.

It took me about a hour and a half to get to St. Cloud and then about fifteen minutes to find the Motel. St. Cloud was so big, when I was a child, it was just a small town, now it was a large city. I went to my room took a shower and then took out the telephone book and started looking up some names. Mom's maiden name was Fizer. I doubted that Florence would still be living, but I remembered Saul, Mom's half brother who was just a couple years older than I was. I found two Saul Fizer in the phone book, and one of them lived in Avon. I dialed the number, a woman answered, and I explained that I was looking for the family of Frances and Florence Fizer. She told me that Saul was their son. I started to tell her that I doubt if Saul would remember me, but I was Lettie's daughter, Patty. I didn't have to say anymore she said that she remembered Saul and the family years ago talking about me and Mom. I told her that I was on vacation and just wanted to see Avon, the farm and the lake that I had loved so much as a child. She invited me to supper that evening and ask me if I could find their place. I told her that I would find it. She went onto say that the farm was no longer there, but that their house was at the end of the road, that the farm had been on.

As I drove toward Avon, I was remembering what the farm and Avon looked like. It was only about twenty or thirty minutes away. I saw the Avon water tower with the name on it and took the off ramp. And there it was the main street. Avon was still small, just one or two main streets, it had maybe a couple new building, but other than that It looked a lot like the old Avon. I drove through the main street, just a couple of blocks and turned right. A couple of blocks and I saw the Catholic Church exactly like it was years ago. Next to it was the schoolhouse the front was built onto the old building, that I had spent part of six grade in. The church was on the corner, not more than a couple hundred feet past the church was Middle Spunk Lake. If you turned right at the church, it would take you around to the beach, if you turned left, it would take you toward where the farm was, about a quarter of a mile. I turned left and everything had changed, the gravel road was now pavement. Along the right side where the lake was, had been farmland years ago that circle the lake, most had belonged to my grandfather. Now were modern homes all around the lake, so close together that it was difficult to see the lake. On the left side, instead of the farmland, that had also belonged to Grandpa, and the town cemetery, there again was modern houses side by side. I could see the cemetery halfway up the street, at one time was called a road, in behind the houses. When I got to the end of the road, I noticed the four-lane highway that had took most of what was at one time the farm. On the left was Saul and Mary Ann's house.

Saul and I spent the evening, after supper talking about our childhood and how much the farm had meant to both of us. Saul told me that his mother, Florence was still living and in a nursing home in Albany. Saul said that his mother would love to see me. I finally said goodbye, after looking at some old pictures of Mom and me on the farm and exchanging address. I went back to St. Cloud, to the motel.

Before I went to bed I called Anna to let her know that I was okay. She said that her Grandpa was okay, but that her Dad was very upset and wanted to talk to me. I gave her my phone number there and told her to tell them I was okay. I went to bed. About midnight the phone rang, the switchboard operator said I had a call, I was pretty sure who it was. Barry told me he didn't understand why I left. I told him if he wanted to talk about it, we could when I got back to West Palms. Before he hung up, he said that he missed me and loved me.

The next morning, I got up early and headed toward Albany, which was about fifteen miles past Avon. I found the nursing home and told them who I wanted to see. They gave me the room number and showed me which direction to go. I walked into the room, there were two elderly ladies, neither resembled the Florence that I remembered. Florence was a large woman, and both of these were very thin and frail looking. I said "Florence" and one of the ladies turned to me and said "yes". I walked over and sat on the side of her bed; she was sitting in a recliner. I told her that when I was a child I stayed with her and my grandpa. She said, "Oh, you must have the wrong person". I asked if she remembered Lettie. And then told her that I was her daughter, Patty. She looked at me and said, "Patty, is that really you." We talked for ten minutes or so, and she began to relate a conversation she remembered that my Grandfather told her when she first married him, before Mom left home. Plus, a few things that was about Mom, that confirmed what I had come to suspect.

Frances told her that a couple years after he and Anna were married, one morning they were sitting at the kitchen table. A friend of Anna's, who had already either entered the convent or was going to, came into the kitchen caring a bundle. When she got to the table, she laid it down and said, " 'Anna, Frances, you have to raise this baby for me.' "

They adopted the baby girl and a couple years later adopted a boy that was maybe four or five years old at the time of adoption. He became Mom's big brother. Florence was elderly, but her long-term memory was good, short-term memory is usually the part that's affected with age. She went on to tell me that her brother had a problem, that of molesting young girls and Mom after her Mother died had begun to swipe things. Not anything big just little thing that she would see laying around and then hide them in her drawer. After about an hour I could see that Florence was getting tired, so I excused myself and left, after thanking her for the conversation.

From there it was a couple hundred miles to Bemidji, Minnesota which held good memories of the summer vacations with Mom and Cecil. As I drove along, I thought of the visit with Florence, and I thought of Sister Bernice. Sister Bernice was a Catholic nun that had wrote Mom faithfully over the years. Mom told me that she had grown up in Avon too. Barry and the kids used to tell me that I sure favored this nun, not to be no relation to her, and then they would say maybe she's your Grandma. Of course I told them that was silly, but as a kid I was told that her biological mother was a nun. Another piece of information she gave me was that this nun was twenty-four, when she had Mom. Also, when

I got back home later and was telling Dad the story, he told me that Mom had told him once that she thought she knew who her real mother was. I also found out later that Sister Bernice was still living and would be ninety-eight this year. The age difference was perfect.

I found the lake where we rented a cabin every year. And had a couple take my picture under Babe the Blue Ox next to Paul Bunyan. I had a picture of me when I was ten standing in the same place. I got back to St. Cloud and went to bed after a very informative and exhausting, but happy day. There was only one fly in the ointment, I wished I could have shared my feelings and thoughts with my family and showed them the places that had meant so much to me over the years.

I spent the next day at the beach in Avon. It hadn't changed much. I have a picture of me on an inner tube at the Avon beach. The only difference I see was the kids now had tailor made floating rafts and tubes. Also, I used to look across the lake and see the farm, now all I seen was houses. I spent the day just enjoying the sites and visiting with the town people. The next morning, I checked out of the motel early, said goodbye to Avon and headed back to Minneapolis. While sitting at the beach I made plans for Minneapolis.

When I got to Minneapolis, I headed for the library that was on Nicolette. It was huge, at least to me it was, it had six or seven floors. I told them I was interested in the history of Minneapolis. I was directed to the sixth floor. I told them I wanted to see anything they had in the late thirties. I was amazed at what I found. There were pictures of the Gateway, Hennipin and Nicolette Avenues, exactly as Dad had described them to me. The barber college where Dad got his hair cut, the cafe where Mom worked right next door and the tavern a couple doors from the cafe, all just as he had told me. The Gateway was directly across the street, where Dad would wait for Mom to get off work. I photocopied all the photos and maybe someday I could get an actual copy of the originals. I was told the copies of the originals were twenty-six dollars. There was one picture that they had dated 1938 of the park at the Gateway, with a man that looked so much like my father, that I couldn't believe it. Later when I showed Dad he said that it could be him, but he doesn't remember it. Finally, I had looked and copied all that I could.

I would have to wait till the next morning to catch the bus home. I spent the remainder of the day looking over Minneapolis, it was a beautiful city. Dad to this day says that Minneapolis has always been his favorite city.

As it got dark, I found I had trouble, I couldn't find a motel room for the night. I ended up sleeping in the car, under a streetlight and with all the windows and doors tightly locked. When the car rental agency opened up, I was there, I had slept in the car parked right beside their door.

In a few hours I was on my way back home. I had learned so much about my family and about myself. At last, I had a connection, I knew about my history, my heritage. To many people this doesn't mean much, but to me it was a part of me.

When I got back in town, Barry was waiting for me. He told me that he didn't understand, but he loved me and would I please come home. I loved him also and we had too many years invested. I knew that maybe he would never understand, but this was where I belonged, where God had placed me.

Dad was also doing okay. He cried and talked of the days when he and Mom lived in Minneapolis, as he looked at the pictures I had brought back.

I went back to work at East View. They wouldn't give me a leave of absence, but they would hire me back. Things soon got back to normal.

In August of last year, 1993, Dad started coughing up blood. He had needed oxygen since his bout with pneumonia, at least half of the time. The doctors, along with myself kept telling him that he needed to stop smoking. But he had smoked for sixty years and said he would rather be dead than stop. He was hospitalized with a blood clot in one of his lungs. He was told to either quit smoking or he wouldn't live much longer. Dad quit but has been on oxygen ever since then.

I found a place within walking distance from my home, in the small community we live in, ten miles from West Palms, and before he came home, we moved him into it. He can no longer drive, so I would take him where he needed to go, to shop. In the last five or six weeks he hasn't been able to even go in a store due to the increasing shortness of breath, so I do most of his shopping for him now.

A few weeks after Dad came home from the hospital, I was coming home after doing some shopping. I was thinking about how bad Dad was getting and I could lose him, when I started crying. The next thing I know I was remembering a time when as a child I was standing in the door and Dad had just brought me home, after being with him. I was crying because I didn't want him to go. It was the last time I saw him, until I was ten. I'd had no memory of ever being with Dad, until then. When I got home I stopped at Dad's and told him of my experience. He was concerned because I had been crying, I tried to explain that tears are not always a bad thing, I had finally remembered my father.

My relationship with Dad hasn't all been easy, especially after the first months. We had went different ways. Dad went the worlds way, partying, drinking, living a life totally dedicated to doing his own thing. Most of his life has been spent making sure that he had whatever it took to make him comfortable. Dad has never considered the spiritual side of life. My life, aside from the earlier emotional problems, has involved my family and my faith in God.

We have had a number of disagreements. Dad's opinion on racial matters differ from mine, he says that they have their own place, I disagree. He believes that money is the most important possession and that it will buy anything or anybody, I disagree, it won't buy real love or peace of mind. Dad calls every male that has long hair, a beard or a number of other things, a jerk. He needed some extra space in his kitchen, so I gave him my white utility table. It had a few rusty places on it, I had always just covered them with place mats. He refused it, saying that he wouldn't have it in his house, and asked me how could I have allowed something like that in my house. On one hand Dad can be so critical and harsh, but then he can also be so loving and tender.

As I sit, here at my typewriter, I'm trying to come up with the words to explain what has happened to me in the last twenty-one months. I still love Dad, and because of him, I now feel a love for Mom that I didn't realize before. The way I feel about Mom now, seems kind of a contradiction. Because of knowing that she did not tell me the truth, about her and Dad. But I think I have a better understanding of Mom now. I believe that while Dad was overseas, Mom met Cecil, and he filled the loneliness that she had. Also remember that according to Florence Mom had some problems herself, as a teenager. I feel that maybe, because of the way Dad remembered her before he left for the service, as a very devout Catholic that didn't drink or smoke, that she could not show him the change in herself. Cecil had introduced her to drinking, dancing and the "fun" things she had never known. After a few months, she found out about Loran and had probably hoped that Dad wouldn't give up, so she went to Loran and tried to intimidate her. Mom just couldn't ask Dad to forgive her, and Dad in his own words said that he was so cocky, he just said that if she didn't want him, okay! For the rest of her life, she never forgot him. And as she went deeper into the bottle, the more she talked of him.

Dad says it is so strange, that he was married to Loran for forty-six years, but thinks of Mom now all the time and how stupid he was for not fighting for her. He states that he believes that he is partly responsible for Mom's problems. If he would have made her face him and tell him to his face that she didn't love him, then things might have been different. But there's no way to know that.

Dad feels that my love toward him has changed. He's right in a way. But his love has also changed. Twenty-one months ago, I loved him as a little girl, that had never known a father's love. I looked at him as I think most little girls look at their fathers, a man that could do no wrong, that could protect me against the whole world. He could see in me, what I believed no one else had ever seen, a wonderful human being and a beautiful daughter. And he made me feel that way. He made me feel that I was that person, not just by his actions, but also by telling me how kind, loving and wonderful I was. But all little girls have to grow up. And as they do, their fathers come off the pedestal.

Fathers also in a sense grow up, or begin to look at their daughters as people. As the months went by, I began to get involved in other activities again, the church, my family, my work. Instead of spending six or more hours a day with Dad, I was spending two or three hours with him. When they are little girls, they are looked at as an extension of themselves. Little girls make their fathers feel important, especially if they are no longer made to feel that they are important in their own home. Dad had lost his rightful place in his home, a number of years ago. I gave him back that feeling of importance, of belonging and being wanted. Which he also gave to me. But it was time for both of us to let go a little. I have learned many things in the last couple years. One thing I knew in my head, but never in my heart, that was, that you can love a person with all your being, but not always like that person. I always believed that if you love a person, you take whatever they do and never complain or get angry. If you do get angry, then you must not really love them. I've spent a lot of my years living with guilt, because I would get angry at one of my children, Barry or a friend and then would hate myself. I would pray and ask Jesus what was wrong with me. Many times, he tried to tell me, sometimes using my family, and sometimes by his word. That I was human and that not only did my family understand, but he did also. Dad and I have gotten angry at each other a number of times, but always, later we tell each other just how much we still do love each other. We might not approve of each other's likes and dislikes, but that doesn't change our love. Shortly after Dad moved down here, he told me he wanted to have a serious talk with me. I was still, down deep, unsure of my father's love. I thought that maybe he wanted to go back to Blue Springs. I didn't need to worry. He wanted to talk to me about what he wanted done when he died. Dad wanted to know if he could be buried next to Mom. I told him not to worry that he would be buried next to her. I know that many people, will not understand how I feel about Dad being buried next to Mom. Dad, when that time comes, would like a double marker placed, with Mom's name on it beside Dad's. I never had them together in life and somehow it seems right for someday them to be together in death. Being a Christian, and knowing that there is a life beyond this life and that there is a heaven and a hell, it hurts when dad tells me, that if there is an afterlife, he wants to be with Mom and if she is in hell that is where he wants to go. I continue to pray for Dad, just as I do for Barry, the girls and our grandchildren.

Also, I understand now why I couldn't accept or believe anybody, could really love me. I believed that unless I measured up to standards that were set by others, I couldn't be accepted. I guess that's why I could accept Gods love and not others. But until I learned to love myself, I couldn't accept love from anybody else. As a born again Christian, I have been told that we are to love God first, family second, everybody else third and ourselves last. And with my low opinion of myself, that theory fit in perfectly. I differ with that now, I love and put God first, as imperfect as I might be Jesus died for me just as I am. And if he loved me that much I must love myself, along with everybody else.

The Lord has been so good to me, He has given me a family that is beyond anything I could have imagined when I was young. Also, He has given me a personal life, as a Christian, as a mother, as a wife, and just as a human being, that I wouldn't trade for anything. I have learned so very much from life, and I hope that some of what I have learned I can pass on to my family, also anybody else that might be able to learn and be helped by my mistakes and my experiences.

From Barry I have learned that just because a person does not know how to show, in everyday ways, love and concern, does not mean they don't love. He has stayed by my side, even though he didn't agree with my decisions. When he thinks no one is noticing, the tenderness is exposed. Once when Briana's dog was accidently killed, because he knew how she would feel, he made up a story that he thought would be easier on her. And then there was the time when we went to see Daniel in Fort Leonardwood, during his basic training, Barry was so very proud of our son, and we all knew it. One of the things that was the most difficult for him, but I know made him so proud, was the three trips he made with our daughters down the aisle in a church and in front of so many people.

Barry has never been able to ask for love or show love. What he feels inside, stays inside, except for the time he was serving the Lord and going to church. Because of this he has never received what he needed from those close to him. As Barry has gotten older, he is realizing that he wants his family to show him that we care, but just gets angry and hurt when he does not get the kind of love he wants. He feels that he is forgotten by those closest to him. Which I believe is not true, it's just that if you spend your whole life never letting people see the real you, there is no way for them to know what you need. I don't believe that anybody really knows another person, or for that matter their own selves. Only the Lord really knows what is in a person, but we could try, a little harder, to let others see the real person inside of us all.

Barry is really himself when in the woods, hunting or cutting firewood. We used to work together, him cutting and me busting, what I could, and then we would load together. I enjoyed the feeling of closeness we shared.

I guess the times with Barry that stand out the most and touched my heart the most, were the times that we were both going to church together. To wake up and hear him praying and crying for someone that he felt needed help. He didn't read very well, so at night I would read the Bible out loud. And the memory of him and Daniel together before Daniel died, praying and in church together at least once, will always be the most special. Barry and I beat the odds. I was told many, many years ago that our marriage wouldn't last. That we were so different. It has not always been easy, but even in this day, a commitment is still a commitment. It is so easy today for people to just give up, instead of fighting for what is right. It takes two I know, but many times all it takes is one to hang in there. Barry never left me, I left him, but he wouldn't take a no for an answer, and I'm thankful now that he didn't.

Daniel, my only son, that is waiting now in a place where we never have to part. Independent, strong and with a mind of his own. There is so many wonderful memories of him. He wanted to do so many things, but for reasons that only the Lord knows he wasn't able to do them. He was such a very proud, and loyal young man. He said once that "a Colan can do anything he really wants to do." Of course, I think he really meant that anybody could, not just a Colan.

Anna is too much like me, I'm afraid. She worries too much about what, she thinks, others think about her, Jaron and the girls. I've never met anybody that hasn't talked about how much she is liked. She has been the quiet one in the family, that is, except for her father. She used to talk about how she would like to work with handicapped kids. With the compassion she has, she would be wonderful at it. I hope someday, with the Lord's help, that maybe she will try to do it. I know she can, if she just will believe in the gift that God has given her.

Briana, I hope and pray she "really" knows just how much I love her and how proud of her I am. She, like Daniel, is so much like her father. She doesn't wear her feelings on the outside, like a lot of us do. I remember how independent she was and still is. For me this was hard, when so many times I would have liked to put my arms around her, I felt that she couldn't except it. Once when she was in the hospital, after surgery, during a visit, Jessie, the girls and I were getting ready to leave. Each one kissed her bye, that is except for me, I stood back. Cindy her oldest, came to me and wanted me to give Briana a hug and kiss goodbye. Briana told her something to the effect, that our family didn't hug and kiss, but we still loved each other. I think the lack of outward show of love is more than just part of our personality. I think a lot of it comes from Barry's and mine experiences when we were young. A lot of our own fear of rejection, we passed on to our children.

When I watch the closeness she has with her family, and not just Briana's family, Anna, and Victoria's also, they have all overcome any reluctance to be themselves. All three of the girls not only love their families but also show that love. The one thing that I feel I didn't do when the children were young, probably because I was so wrapped up in my own feelings of inferiority and isolation.

Victoria is our baby, and even though she does not like that distinction, it does not change the fact that she is our youngest, our baby. I think because she was with us longer, it has been harder to let go of her. When I say let go, I mean in our hearts, because we could never try to hold our children in a place where they didn't want to be. I feel that she is probably the most independent of our children, except maybe Daniel. She has ·her own ideas and will make her own way, with or without anyone's help. My prayer for Victoria is that she always remembers that while what others think might not matter in eternity, to always make sure that what ever she does passes the white glove test with the Lord. Of course, that goes for all my children.

There's been a number of times that we have felt lonesome fore our children and Barry at times feels that they don't seem to need us like we do them, which saddens him more. But at those times I remind him that if nothing else we have done right, we have somehow instilled in them the ability to make it on their own, because someday we will be gone. And to remember to take Jesus with them wherever they go or whatever they do.

As I end this, I want to thank the Lord again for what he has done for me. Since I have found Dad I realize what I might have been like, if my early life would have been like I would have wanted it. I might never have found Jesus like I did, had never come to know him as my personal savior and friend. I might never have had the wonderful children I have. I have had experiences, good and bad, that has taught me so much about life. Jesus took the bad that Satan instigated and used it to help teach me things I could not have learned any other way.

I plan on rewriting this if I am given the time, with some changes in names, events and places. I hope my children will understand their mother a little more and be able to see why finding Dad has meant so much to me. He can be a very difficult man, but all those years there has been a very lonely little girl that had some awful big problems, that she has finally found some answers to.

~Patty

Bonus Material

Poetry

By Patricia Morrison – Collins

Dad

Dad, forty-five years in all, have come and gone
since that time in the hall.
I was ten and had to be strong
as you turned from my heart's call.
A family I had, and as they grew
I wondered, Dad, what you would think
if you only knew.
And then, in October of '92,
united at last with a love so strong.
We learned together how to erase
the years gone wrong.
But alas, Dad, as you and I were to see
we never know what tomorrow will be.
For after two short years, with memories and tears
with your hand in mine, on wings of love
your soul was carried to that land above.
We, your grandchildren and I
knew that again we would meet
for in those two short years
you learned of a love that would keep us near.
Not only did you learn of the love
of grandchildren, daughter, and son-in-law too,
you also found a Savior's love that
would lead you to that land above.
You told me to be strong, and not to cry
that Danny you would see
and there await however long
when united forever, we would be.
So here I am learning once again
to be strong, until the time we
meet again and walk hand in hand
to see the wonders of that promised land.

MUST I

Sixteen years ago, a summons went out,

A son was called home and I had to shout

Too soon, too soon, it must not be, but alas, it was, and we shall see

That time went on, and to remember,

Became a means that made it kinder. But now, at this time in my life, I see a concern that

spells trouble for me.

For now you see, again I said too soon,
Too soon it must not be

This time a Father it was, that a summons came.
Some said old he was and though it's a shame however,

in our heart of hearts, With forty-one years apart, Daddy was thirty-six and I was ten, We
loved each other as we had then

Some say, be oh so thankful for what you had,

For you may have never known your dad

And though I see the truth they speak, I also know that I miss a dad, so sweet

Memories so cherished flood my mind,

But the memories bring pain to this heart of mine,

For memories cannot replace the touch of a Father that meant so very much.

Time heals all pain, I've been told.

What of memories, will they unfold, or will I, as seasons pass, forget the touch that meant so

much? Nay, I shall not forget, for I'd rather have the pain of heart than let the memories depart.

For in my family, my Son I see, and for many years we were a family.

Only two years we had, my Father and I, and only memories I will have until I die.
And then not only will I see my Lord, but I will also be with my son and father.

What Do You See

When you look at me, what do you see? Do you see the dreams, dreams filled with sunshine and moonbeams? Do you see the hand that wants to reach into the land, to the sad, destitute, and poor, to find and open the door that will give them reason and more?

When you look at me, what do you see? Do you see the visions in my eye when I look into the blue, blue sky? The magnificence and wonder as I search and ponder just what lies beyond my eye and how it will be when I say goodbye.

When you look at me, what do you see? Do you see the love that aches inside, like an evergreen clove within the flower it hides? For like a flower so delicate, the petals will fall, for ridicule causes pain and mockery builds a wall.

When you look at me, what do you see? Did you see the child that lived within, A child that felt she would never love again,

For love like a flower needs nurturing to grow,
Without understanding and care it loses its glow.

When you look at me, what do you see? Do you see a father who listened and let me be me, for he took the time to love the real me? Only two years were allowed to love and know each in a way that words cannot tell.

Friend or Foe

It seems to be closing in; I can sense its nearness reaching, always reaching, never satisfied—turbulent at times, haunted as if possessed, frequented by phantoms of the deep. Set apart from the rest of the living. But wait! There, sitting atop, in the midst of the fog like a watchman, it displaces the darkness —That one lone beam in the night.

As I slowly move toward it in the quiet of the early morning darkness, before the dawn, it continues to roar and moves further toward me. Its white tentacles grasp for more and more. Its seductiveness I cannot resist; I continue to move toward it. That beam in the night shows me the way, my feet sinking with every step. Then I hear it: "Come, come, come." "Yes, yes, I hear you." As I look back to see my footprints in the sand, I must retreat or it will take me. I hear a distant warning: "Run, run, run." I retreat, but as I retrace my steps, I feel it pulling me back. There's a sense of belonging, an empathy between us.

They're right on the edge as it reaches for me. I see the tiny white Jonathan seagull. Just as the white tentacles reach to claim another prize, Jonathan spreads his beautiful wings and takes to the air. It's funny how it seems to stop just short of claiming more and more space, but at the same time, it is inching ever closer and closer. Then I see the light of day and I know that a new day is dawning and see a new light on things to come.

There Was A Woman

There was a woman, Maria was her name, misplaced and unsure of her fame.
She gave her love to the four-footed kind; mortal love never
seemed she able to find.
She searched and searched everywhere, trying to find someone
to share her life.
The answer lay within her own soul,
but her heart she knew could never be whole.
For her mother and father were not her own, which made her feel
very alone.
Instead, in a bottle her soul came to abide, for in the bottle from
the truth she could hide.
Suspicious and bitter her life became;
such a loss it was, really a shame.
For a wee small child was standing
aside, waiting for her love to come and
abide. This woman full of pain and doubt
turned her back on a tender sprout.

Unable to give of her love and tender care,
to this child she gave the best of material fare
This child she believed could never be,
more than what she could see
Her lot in life she put the blame,
on this child and made her lame

In a drunken state, at age of twelve this child so dear,
she called a whore and gave a slap, without a fear
Still at another time, despondent and alone,
smelling of drink she would try to atone
Without a thought said she, you were never wanted by he,
my father you see, that according to mother never loved me

She taught this child, in life to play the part,
but never gave her the tools of the heart

Dad

Mom

Dad told me during our first days together that I would cry for him not to take me home I wanted to stay with him. It got harder & harder for him to pick me up & then leave me crying back at moms.

Right below the Barber shop sign is a cafe that is where mom worked when she met Dad. The Gateway building is right across the street from the cafe area.

This was took in 1938, when Dad was in Minneapolis & met mom. We're not positive, but we think this is him — The original copy is better.

The Gateway building, that was a tourist travelers information center

The Gateway District, 1930's

Disclaimer:

All photos of Minneapolis were acquired from public domain.

Author bio
Welcome To My World

Time flies, sun rises, and shadows fall.
Let time go by, love is forever overall.
From an English sundial.

Hi, I'm Egatireh. Egatireh is "Heritage" spelled backwards. I chose this name because of my strong belief in a person's heritage. Where we have come from and above all where we are going. Next to my faith in Jesus Christ, my family is the most important aspect of my life.

I married at the age of 14 and am still married to the same man. I had four children: a son who was taken from this world by cancer at the age of 21, three daughters, seven grandchildren, and one great-grandchild.

Bio Update:

My mom is now 84.

We lost our dad about 9 years ago.

They were married 62 years.

Mom is a great-great-grandmother now

And has 9 great-grandchildren.

~Vonda Almond

Made in the USA
Columbia, SC
04 July 2025